TAHERA RAWJI and HAMIDA SULEI

simply INDIAN

SWEET AND SPICY RECIPES FROM INDIA, PAKISTAN AND EAST AFRICA

whitecap

Sixth Printing, 2009

Edited by Lesley Cameron
Copy edited by Marial Shea
Cover design by Jane Lightle and Roberta Batchelor
Food photographs by Jenn Walton/Digiwerx Studio
Food styling by JoAnne Strongman/JMS Food Styling and Design
Interior design and illustrations by Warren Clark

Tahera Rawji would like to thank Rukhsana, Nusrat, Bindu and NoorZehra for assisting in preparing food for the photo shoot. She would like to thank Manek, Rukhsana, Bindu, Chandrika, Gita and Pushpa for providing dishes and silverware for the photo shoot.

Printed and bound in Canada

National Library of Canada Cataloguing in Publication Data

Rawji, Tahera.
    Simply Indian : sweet and spicy recipes from India, Pakistan and East Africa / Tahera Rawji, Hamida Suleman

ISBN 1-55285-411-6
ISBN 978-1-55285-411-2

    1. Cookery, Indic. 2. Cookery, Pakistani. 3. Cookery, African.
I. Suleman, Hamida. II. Title.
TX724.5.I5R38 2003   641.5954   C2003-910245-9

The publisher acknowledges the support of the Canada Council for the Arts and the Cultural Services Branch of the Government of British Columbia for our publishing program. We acknowledge the financial support of the Government of Canada through the Book Publishing Industry Development Program for our publishing activities.

Contents

Acknowledgments

I would like to thank the following people without whom this cookbook of home-tested recipes would not be possible: my husband Shaukat, daughter Safinaaz, son Zuher and son-in-law Akil who happily accepted the job as taste testers. Bindu, Meera, Rukhsana and Nusrat who stood by me 100% at all times. Last but certainly not least, my Dad, Mom and sister Jenny for their love and encouragement.

—Tahera Rawji

I would like to thank all the members of my family, especially my husband Mohamed, son Kazim, son-in-law Sibtain, daughter Fatima, daughter-in-law Aarifa and all my grandchildren for all their love, support and encouragement. I would also like to give sincere thanks to all my sisters, brothers, and my Mom and Dad too.

Many thanks to my friend Tahera Rawji, an expert in cooking. It has been a great pleasure to be associated with her in this venture to produce our first cookbook.

—Hamida Suleman

Introduction

Born and raised in East Africa, **Tahera Rawji** studied in Nairobi, Kenya at the Institute of Domestic Arts in 1972 before moving to Canada. Tahera has shared the secrets of the exotic dishes of Pakistan, India and southern India in her cooking classes for over six years.

A wide variety of food exists in India today, ranging from the smokey clay-oven roasted tandoori chicken and biryanis of the Moguls to the fish and prawn curries of the Madras. Both vegetarian and non-vegetarian dishes capture the intricacies of Indian cuisine. As well, this book brings together various Gujarati dishes very popular in the state of Gujarat to represent the Indian cuisine.

For Tahera there is much satisfaction in seeing the smiles on the faces of her students rather than just trying to teach them to follow a recipe. She was encouraged to write a cookbook by most of her friends and her students who took her course repeatedly to broaden their knowledge of Indian cooking.

The recipes in this book have been written with easy-to-follow steps designed to help you and your family enjoy delicious meals every day or on special occasions. Always remember the basic rule in Indian cooking—the slower you cook, the better it tastes. And always gather all your ingredients together before starting to cook.

The recipes do not always follow strictly traditional methods but the taste is always 100% authentic. All these recipes have been tried on friends, relatives and students who live here and abroad and everyone was more than satisfied with the authenticity of the meals. Enjoy this culinary adventure.

Hamida Suleman developed her love of cooking at a very early age, when still in school in East Africa. Later, encouraged greatly by her husband, children, grandchildren, nieces and nephew, she won an award in a cooking competition held by the Ladies Union in Dar-es-Salaam.

Before coming to Canada, Hamida spent some time in Dubai, where she gave cooking lessons and demonstrations. Many of her students have been impatiently awaiting this book.

Indian desserts are normally rich, creamy and very sweet. Hamida has included a few simple dessert recipes for the more adventurous cooks who would like to give them a try. They say "the way to a man's heart is through his stomach" and with the recipes we have compiled for you in this book, you are sure to get to your man's stomach with no trouble at all. The next stage is up to you!

Most recipes give serving suggestions including breads and salads. This should help you enjoy your meal with that extra little touch of authenticity.

Simply Indian

Before You Begin

The Right Way to Do Chasni (Sugar Syrup)

A concentrated solution of sugar and water is called chasni or syrup. The sugar and water are heated slowly so that the water does not boil before the sugar has dissolved. You must stir gently at this stage. Once all the sugar has dissolved it can be brought to a boil *but not stirred*.

Chasni has various strengths or degrees. A mild one does not thread when pressed between thumb and forefinger, it just leaves a syrup imprint. The second strength is when the chasni thickens and, when tested between thumb and forefinger, forms 1 thread. The third strength is when it gives 2 to 3 threads. This stage is also known as the soft ball consistency. When a little bit is dropped in cool water it turns into a soft ball. The last stage is the hard ball, when it almost caramelizes.

To Measure Butter or Margarine

To measure butter or margarine in a cup, do not melt it and then measure. If the recipe calls for half a cup of butter or margarine, take a measuring jug and fill with water to the half-cup level, then add enough butter so that the water reaches the 1-cup level. Drain off the water and use the butter as required.

Preparing Chicken

When preparing chicken, always remove the skin and excess fat under the skin and on the flesh. Small chickens are tender and deliciously moist when properly cooked. If you prefer to debone your chicken before adding it to a dish, then go ahead and do it. I prefer to leave it on the bone. For recipes requiring cut-up chicken, I simply cut right through the bones. If a recipe indicates that the chicken should be in curry size pieces, it means 3 inch (7.5 centimetre) square pieces.

Rice and Beans

Always wash rice before cooking to remove dirt or grit. Then soak it in double the volume of water for half an hour. Do not change the water more than twice as rice tends to break easily. Beans should be washed twice to remove dust and dirt. Then they should be soaked in fresh water for at least 2 hours. I usually soak my beans overnight as that helps them to cook faster. Do not soak beans for more than 10 hours as they will begin to ferment.

Additions to Curries

Coconut Milk:
Add to curry and bring to a boil over low heat. Once boiling, lower to a simmer again. The best flavor is achieved by not overcooking it. If the oil of the coconut milk surfaces to the top, it changes the flavor and creates an extra greasiness.

Yogurt:
For best results, always use plain, unsweetened yogurt with a slightly sour flavor, unless the recipe specifies otherwise. When adding to curry, bring to a boil slowly, stirring occasionally. Once it has boiled, it may be cooked on slightly high heat if the recipe calls for it.

Clarified Butter or Ghee

Clarified butter can be made by taking margarine and butter in equal proportions and heating over low heat with 2 pods of cardamom. Heat for at least 1 hour. This will leave the milk solids to settle at the bottom with the clear butter on top. Scoop out as much clear butter as you can. Transfer it into a glass jar and store in the refrigerator for up to 6 months.

Serving Indian Food

Eating habits vary drastically across India. Probably no other country in the world has such a variety of foods and eating patterns.

In the North, rice is eaten first with some lentils, then a chapati with a dry meat dish. In the South, where rice is the staple dish, it is eaten with different coconut-flavored curries. In other places a sweet dish is consumed first alongside the rest of the food.

I am sure people from the West who are invited to Indian homes for a meal always remark on the amount of food served and the large quantities of oil, spices and rich desserts.

In almost all the recipes, we have noted accompaniments for each particular dish to make your meal as enjoyable as possible.

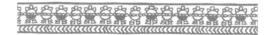

Pantry Basics

Garam Masala

Garam Masala is a combination of different hot spices ground together. It can be bought in Indian stores in packages but it is not the same as making your own. Garam Masala is used in most curried, dried or braised dishes and usually added at the end of cooking just before serving. Ground garam masala will keep for about 1 year.

Garam Masala—Fragrance 1

1/2 cup	cardamom pods	120 mL
3	nutmegs	3
1 Tbsp.	black pepper	15 mL
6	star anise	6
1/4 cup	cinnamon sticks	60 mL

Garam Masala—Fragrance 2

1/2 cup	cardamom green pods	120 mL
2 Tbsp.	black pepper	30 mL
1 Tbsp.	ground cloves	15 mL
1 cup	cinnamon sticks	240 mL
1/4 cup	fennel seeds	60 mL
2	nutmegs	2

1. In a small pan dry roast the spices for fragrance 1 or 2 over very low heat for about 1 minute.
2. Let cool for 5 minutes.
3. Grind to a fine powder in a coffee grinder.
4. Store in an airtight jar on your spice rack.

Grinding Tip
Grinding spices with a mortar and pestle is certainly authentic and traditional, but it is also time-consuming and labor intensive! I use a coffee grinder to grind my spices. Just be sure you keep the grinder separate and use it only for this specific purpose. Otherwise your coffee may never taste the same again!

Whole Garam Masala

This is used to spice up rice while boiling.

12	whole cloves	12
4	sticks cinnamon 2 inches (5 cm) long	4
2	nutmegs (broken into small pieces)	2
2	star anise (broken into small pieces)	2
8	cardamom pods	8
18	black peppercorns	18

Put all the ingredients in an airtight jar and keep it on your spice rack. It will keep for more than a year.

Whole Garam Masala is usually used to flavor rice and is also used in some curries.

Fijian Mixed Spice

½ cup	aniseed	120 mL
1 Tbsp.	cardamom	15 mL
1 Tbsp.	cloves	15 mL
½ cup	star flower	120 mL
½ cup	cinnamon sticks	120 mL
8	black peppercorns	8

1. Dry roast each ingredient separately in a frying pan until golden brown.
2. Let cool for 5 minutes.
3. Grind to a fine powder in a coffee grinder.
4. Store in an airtight jar on your spice rack.

Fijian Spice Masala

¾ cup	fennel seeds	180 mL
3 Tbsp.	cardamom seeds	45 mL
3 Tbsp.	cloves	45 mL
14	black peppercorns	14
1 cup	cinnamon sticks	240 mL
¾ cup	star anise	180 mL

1. Dry roast all the above ingredients separately in a frying pan until golden brown.
2. Allow to cool for 5 minutes.
3. Grind in coffee grinder.
4. Store in an airtight jar on your spice rack.

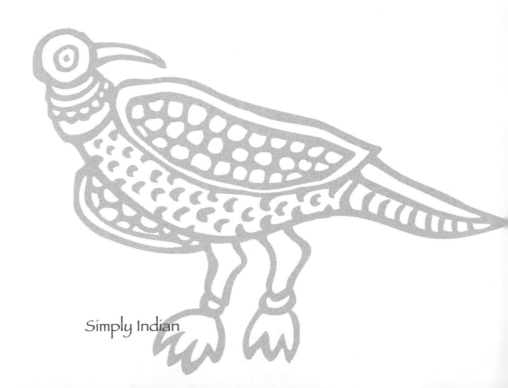

Simply Indian

List of Staple Ingredients

Aalu	Potatoes
Ajwain	Carom or tymol seeds
Atta	Chapati flour or wheat flour
Baigan	Eggplant or brinjal
Bhindi	Okra
Channa	Whole gram or chickpeas
Channa flour	Gram flour or chickpea flour
Dahi	Yogurt
Dalchini	Cinnamon
Dhana Jeera	Coriander and cumin powder
Dhania	Coriander leaves
Falooda noodles	China grass or agar agar
Goover	Flat Indian beans
Haldi	Turmeric
Hing	Asafoetida
Ilaichi	Cardamom
Imli	Tamarind
Jeera	Cumin
Kala jeera	Black cumin seeds
Kalonji	Onion seeds
Karela	Bitter gourd
Kewra essence	Essence of paradanus ordorstismus
Khuskhus	Poppy seeds

Kofta	Meatballs
Lasan	Garlic
Limro	Curry leaves
Maizena	Maize flour or corn starch
Masoor daal	Orange lentils
Mattar	Peas
Methi	Fenugreek
Mircha	Chilies
Mircha lal	Red chilies
Mircha mota	Green bell peppers
Mung daal	Green split lentils
Palak	Spinach
Phoodina	Mint
Pista	Pistachio nuts
Rai	Black mustard seeds
Shah jeera	Black cumin seeds
Sooji	Cream of wheat or semolina
Toor daals	Split pigeon peas
Tukhmari	Tulsi seeds
Urad daal	Black split gram or split mah lentils

List of Staple Ingredients

Soups and Snacks

This chapter includes both vegetarian and non-vegetarian soups. The vegetarian soups are more popular in southern India and are used for people recovering after various illnesses. If you like your soup spicy, you can add some chilies.

All kinds of snacks and savories are prepared in the Indian kitchen. The social cup of tea or coffee is always accompanied by a variety of snacks such as samosas, bajiyas, pakoras or kebabs. There are many types of appetizers and snacks in Indian cuisine. They range from simple tidbits to quite elaborate delicacies that require significant preparation. It is not possible to name them all—and the recipes for them would fill an entire cookbook!

Try serving some of the appetizers listed in the following pages at your next party and wait for the compliments to flow from your guests.

Chicken Soup with Barley and Vegetables

½ lb.	chicken breasts	250 g
4 cups	water	950 mL
½ cup	barley (rinsed)	120 mL
2	bay leaves	2
1	cinnamon stick, ½ inch (1.2 cm) long	1
1½ tsp.	garlic paste	2.5 mL
1½ tsp.	ginger paste	2.5 mL
1	large carrot (chopped)	1
1	large onion (chopped)	1
1	large potato (peeled and cubed)	1
½ cup	parsley (chopped)	120 mL
½ tsp.	salt	2.5 mL
½ tsp.	black pepper	2.5 mL

Garlic and ginger pastes can be found in most East Indian grocery stores and regular supermarkets.

My grandchildren, Ammar, Mohammad and Mehdiya, tell me this is their favorite soup. It gives children a quick nourishing boost after a long and tiring day at school. The cinnamon stick adds a certain special something to the taste.

When I prepare this soup at home, I usually use coarsely ground fresh pepper to give it a zingy taste.

1. Remove skin and fat from the chicken and cut into small cubes (see page viii).
2. In a saucepan add the chicken, water, barley, bay leaves, cinnamon stick, garlic paste and ginger paste.
3. Bring to a boil and cook for half an hour. Then add the chopped carrot, onion and potato.
4. Simmer for 10 minutes or until tender.
5. Stir in the parsley, salt and pepper.
6. Remove cinnamon stick and bay leaves.

Serve hot with bread or tandoori roti.

Serves 6–8

Pea Soup with Meat

What could be more welcoming than a bowl of freshly made pea soup with chunks of meat? Hearty soups like this one are especially good on cold winter nights. You may use chicken instead of beef if you wish. To make it hot, add a couple of green chilies when bringing the meat to boil.

1. Boil peas in 2 cups (475 mL) of water until done (approximately 20–25 minutes).
2. Boil the beef in the 4 cups (950 mL) of water until tender (approximately 20–25 minutes), then cut into 2-inch (5-cm) cubes. Set aside 2 cups (475 mL) of the broth.
3. In a saucepan, combine the beef with the remaining broth and undrained peas.
4. Boil rice in another saucepan in 2 cups of water (475 mL) until cooked, then drain.
5. Add the boiled rice and onions to the broth.
6. Add salt, pepper and melted butter.
7. Simmer for 10 minutes.
8. Add the toasted pita pieces just before serving.

Serve hot.

Serves 5

¼ cup	dried peas (soaked overnight, drained and rinsed)	60 mL
2 cups	water	475 mL
1 lb.	shin of beef	455 g
4 cups	water	950 mL
¼ cup	rice	60 mL
4	onions (sliced)	4
½ tsp.	salt	2.5 mL
½ tsp.	black pepper	2.5 mL
1 Tbsp.	melted butter	15 mL
1	toasted crisp pita bread (cut in small pieces)	1

Soups and Snacks

Pumpkin Soup

1 lb.	shin of beef (with bones)	455 g
½ tsp.	ginger (crushed)	2.5 mL
½ tsp.	garlic (crushed)	2.5 mL
¼	small pumpkin (peeled and cut)	¼
2 Tbsp.	butter	30 mL
3 oz.	all-purpose flour	85 g
1	sprig of parsley	1
¼ tsp.	black pepper (ground)	1.2 mL
1 Tbsp.	salt	15 mL

*P*ieces of boiled pumpkin can be served alongside this soup if desired. You may use chicken and chicken broth instead of shin of beef. Instead of pumpkin, you may use any other squash.

1. Cut meat into small shreds and boil with the ginger, garlic and bones for approximately 20 minutes.
2. Add pumpkin and cook slowly until meat is done (approximately 30 minutes).
3. Set aside 1 ½ cups of broth (360 mL) from the stock.
4. Melt butter in a small saucepan. Add flour and fry until brown.
5. Add the reserved meat broth and stir well to thicken.
6. Now add the broth to the meat and pumpkin mixture.
7. Finely chop the parsley. Add to the soup and simmer for 15 minutes.
8. Add salt and pepper to taste.

Serve hot.

Serves 5

Spinach Bone Soup

*T*he spinach and tomatoes give this soup a lovely rich flavor.

1. In a large pot, bring the lamb to a boil in the water. Add salt and cook for about 30 minutes or until the lamb is done.
2. Add the spinach, tomatoes and onions. Simmer for another 10 minutes or until the stock thickens.
3. Remove pot from heat. Separate the bones from the stock and discard the bones. Use a hand-held blender to blend the soup.
4. Now pour in the cream, sprinkle with pepper and jeera and serve hot.

Serve with crispy pita bread.

Serves 4

1 lb.	lamb with bones in (shin of lamb preferred)	455 g
3 cups	water	720 mL
½ tsp.	salt	2.5 mL
1	bunch of spinach (cleaned and chopped)	1
2	large tomatoes (peeled and chopped)	2
1	medium onion (sliced)	1
1 Tbsp.	heavy cream	15 mL
½ tsp.	ground black pepper	2.5 mL
½ tsp.	jeera (cumin seeds) (crushed)	2.5 mL

Spinach Soup

1 lb.	stewing beef with marrow bones (optional)	455 g
2 cups	water	475 mL
2	medium onions (finely chopped)	2
1	large bunch of spinach (cleaned and chopped)	1
¼ cup	rice	60 mL
1 cup	water	240 mL
½ tsp.	garlic (crushed)	2.5 mL
1	bunch of cilantro (chopped)	1
½ tsp.	salt	2.5 mL
2 Tbsp.	butter	30 mL
2 tsp.	Tabasco sauce	10 mL

Hearty soups like this one are especially good when the evenings are cool in early fall. This recipe is an old family favorite.

1. Cut meat into small cubes and boil with 2 cups (475 mL) of water in a large saucepan for approximately 25 minutes.
2. In a separate pot, boil the onions and spinach. When the vegetables are tender, drain then purée with a potato masher or hand-held blender. Return to the pot.
3. Boil the rice in 1 cup (240 mL) of water for 10–15 minutes. When done, add the rice, meat and stock to the mashed vegetables.
4. Add the crushed garlic, chopped cilantro, salt, butter and Tabasco.
5. Simmer for 10–15 minutes.

Serve hot with naan or parathas.

Serves 5

Kasta Kachori

This is my own recipe and my daughter Safinaaz's favorite. Kasta Kachori can be made ahead of time and reheated in the oven. They are often served as appetizers.

1. Part-boil the mung daal in the 2 ½ cups (600 mL) water for 7 minutes and put aside.
2. In a bowl, add the flour, salt, 2 Tbsp. (30 mL) of the oil and the yogurt and work into a smooth, springy dough. Set aside.
3. For vaghar (tempering), heat the remaining oil on medium high heat. Add the mustard seeds and curry leaves. Let them crack to produce an aroma.
4. Add the green chilies, shredded cabbage, ground cumin, garlic paste and turmeric. Combine and add to lentil mixture. Cook for one minute then remove from heat.
5. Apply butter or oil to your hands and shape the dough into 6 rounds 3 inches (7.5 cm) in diameter. Place a little lentil mixture in the center, fold over, damp the edges to seal and shape them round again.
6. Flatten out into pancakes about ¼ inch (.6 cm) thick and 3 inches (7.5 cm) diameter.
7. Deep-fry and drain. Serve hot or cold.

Makes 6

½ cup	mung daal (soaked overnight in cold water, drained and rinsed)	120 mL
2 ½ cups	water	600 mL
3 cups	all-purpose flour	720 mL
1 tsp.	salt	5 mL
6 Tbsp.	vegetable oil	90 mL
1 ¼ cups	yogurt	300 mL
¼ tsp.	rai (black mustard seeds)	1.2 mL
1 tsp.	limro (curry leaves)	5 mL
1 Tbsp.	green chilies (chopped)	15 mL
¼	small cabbage (shredded)	¼
¼ tsp.	jeera (ground cumin)	1.2 mL
¼ tsp.	garlic paste	1.2 mL
¼ tsp.	haldi (turmeric)	1.2 mL
	vegetable oil for deep-frying	

Pakoras (Dumplings with Vegetables)

2 ½ cups	gram flour (sifted)	600 mL
½	bunch of spinach (chopped)	½
1 Tbsp.	chopped cilantro	15 mL
1	medium potato (chopped)	1
1	medium onion (chopped)	1
	few pieces of cauliflower	
¼ tsp.	dhania (coriander seeds) (split)	1.2 mL
¼ tsp.	salt	1.2 mL
¼ tsp.	chili powder	1.2 mL
¼ tsp.	garlic (crushed)	1.2 mL
¼ tsp.	Eno fruit salt	1.2 mL
3–4 cups	vegetable oil for deep-frying	720–950 mL

*P*akoras are the most common appetizer in the Punjab state in northern India. If made in advance, they can be three-quarters cooked, kept at room temperature, then refried again just before serving. When prepared this way, they will be a little crispier than usual. The nice thing about these is that they can be adapted to your own taste by using shrimp, chicken, or even paneer instead of vegetables. When doing this, always remember to increase the amount of coriander seeds and garlic to ½ tsp. (2.5 mL). This is done to ceromatize them and give them a zingy taste.

1. In a large bowl, mix together the flour, spinach, cilantro, potato, onion, cauliflower, coriander seeds, salt, chili powder and garlic.
2. Use a tablespoon to add water little by little to form a thick paste.
3. Add the fruit salt.
4. Heat the oil in a large pot.
5. Form the paste into balls and slowly deep-fry them.

Serve with chutney of your choice (pages 89–96).

Makes 6

Idli

Idli will stimulate anybody's taste buds. My friend Bindu and I enjoy it with a tangy slice of lemon and a side serving of salad. On special occasions it makes an excellent accompaniment to other vegetable dishes.

1. Microwave the frozen vegetables and chop finely.
2. Add ginger and green chili to the chopped vegetables. Set aside.
3. In a saucepan fry the mustard seeds in 3 Tbsp. (45 mL) of the vegetable oil. Add the curry leaves and vegetable mix and continue frying for 2 minutes.
4. In another large saucepan, heat the remaining 3 Tbsp. (45 mL) of vegetable oil on medium high, add the cream of wheat and fry for 3 minutes, stirring continuously. Add the butter.
5. Now add the vegetable mixture to this large saucepan. Remove from the heat and let cool for 5–10 minutes.
6. Add the buttermilk and salt and leave for 3–4 hours to ferment.
7. Now add 1 tsp. (5 mL) of baking powder to the ingredients in the saucepan and mix well.
8. You may have to add buttermilk if the mixture has thickened too much. Add the cilantro once the batter is ready.
9. For the steaming stage, heat water in a large pan.
10. Grease the Idli pan and pour in the batter (not more than 2 Tbsp./30 mL at a time). Steam over the large saucepan for 10 minutes.
11. Repeat until the batter is finished.

Serve with sambaal curry and Coconut Chutney (page 90).

Makes 6

½ cup	frozen mixed vegetables	120 mL
1 inch	piece ginger (chopped)	2.5 cm
1	green chili (chopped)	1
½ tsp.	rai (black mustard seeds)	2.5 mL
6 Tbsp.	vegetable oil	90 mL
1 Tbsp.	limro (curry leaves)	15 mL
2 ½ cups	sooji (cream of wheat)	600 mL
2 oz.	butter	55 g
1 tsp.	salt	5 mL
6 cups	buttermilk	1.5 L
1 tsp.	baking powder	5 mL
1	cilantro sprig (chopped)	1
	Idli pan for steaming	

An Idli pan is a must for steaming the Idlis. There is no substitute for it, but the pans are found in almost all East Indian grocery stores.

Puris and Wada Chaat

1 cup	urad daal	240 mL
1 ½ tsp.	salt	7.5 mL
½ cup	oil for deep-frying	120 mL
4 cups	yogurt	950 mL
1 tsp.	sugar	5 mL
1 lb.	flat crispy puris or Doritos (or any crispy potato chips)	455 g
2	small potatoes (peeled, boiled, and cubed)	2
2 Tbsp.	Podina Chutney (see page 92)	30 mL
2 Tbsp.	Tamarind Chutney (see page 94)	30 mL
2 Tbsp.	Red Chili Chutney (see page 96)	30 mL
2 tsp.	jeera (cumin seeds) (crushed)	10 mL
1 tsp.	chili powder	5 mL
½ tsp.	roasted chili powder (or to taste)	2.5 mL
1 inch	piece ginger (finely sliced)	2.5 cm

Hot and spicy would be the best way of describing this mouthwatering Gujarati dish. Wadas are dumplings fried in hot oil and they can be made a few hours ahead. This is a great vegetable side dish.

1. To make the wada: wash the urad daal and soak overnight in cold water.
2. The following day, drain the daal and grind it in a blender, gradually mixing in enough water to make a thick batter. Add 1 tsp. (5 mL) of the salt.
3. Heat enough oil in a wok for deep-frying. Drop tablespoonfuls of the batter into the hot oil.
4. Fry until light golden then remove and place in hot water for three minutes.
5. Remove from hot water and gently squeeze out as much water as you can without losing the shape of the wada.
6. Beat the yogurt well with the remaining ½ tsp. (2.5 mL) salt and the sugar.
7. To serve, put a few wada, puri and potato cubes on each plate. Top with yogurt and ½ tsp. (2.5 mL) of all the chutneys and sprinkle with a little salt, cumin, chili powder, roasted chili powder and ginger slices. Top with crispy puri (crunched into crumbs) and serve immediately.

Serves 5

Bhajiya (Black-Eyed Bean Dumplings)

A must-have dish for the holy month of Ramadan, Bhajiyas are never left over after any meal. They taste wonderful with chutney (pages 89–96)—our family's favorite is Coconut Chutney (page 90).

1. Soak beans in cold water overnight. Drain and rinse in clean water the next day. The husk will come off, leaving the split beans looking nice and clean.
2. Blend the beans and onion in a blender until they become smooth and fine. Add a little water if necessary. Be careful not to add too much water as the mixture has to be in a paste form.
3. Add all the spices, the salt and the baking powder and mix thoroughly. Leave to marinate for 6 hours.
4. Heat oil in a wok for deep-frying. With one hand, form the mix into balls and deep-fry slowly until nice and crispy and golden brown.

Serve hot or cold.

Makes 16

2 ½ cups	split black-eyed beans (soaked overnight)	600 mL
1	small onion (chopped)	1
¼ tsp.	ginger (crushed)	1.2 mL
¼ tsp.	garlic (crushed)	1.2 mL
1 Tbsp.	cilantro (chopped)	15 mL
1 tsp.	haldi (turmeric)	5 mL
¼ tsp.	chili (chopped)	1.2 mL
¼ tsp.	salt	1.2 mL
¼ tsp.	baking powder	1.2 mL
2 cups	vegetable oil	475 mL

Spinach and Black-Eyed Bean Soup

3 cups	water	720 mL
³⁄₄ cup	black-eyed beans (soaked overnight)	180 mL
½ tsp.	salt	2.5 mL
½ tsp.	haldi (turmeric)	2.5 mL
1	bunch of spinach (cleaned and chopped)	1
2 inches	ginger root (grated)	5 cm
½ tsp.	red chili powder	2.5 mL
2 Tbsp.	butter	30 mL
1	medium onion (chopped)	1
½ tsp.	garlic (crushed)	2.5 mL
½ tsp.	jeera (cumin seeds)	2.5 mL

A deceptively simple soup that can be made a day ahead. It can also be refrigerated for 2 days.

1. Put the water in a large saucepan and bring to a boil. Add the soaked beans, salt and turmeric and cook for 45 minutes, uncovered.
2. Add the spinach, ginger and red chili powder and cook for a further 20 minutes.
3. Add more water if necessary.
4. In a frying pan, melt the butter and cook the onion, garlic and cumin seeds until golden brown.
5. Pour this over the bean mixture.

Serve hot.

Serves 5

Simply Indian

Vegetable Soup

A healthy soup with plenty of vegetables. You can experiment with your own choice of vegetables but be sure not to omit the English parsley as that's what really enhances the flavor.

1. Chop all the vegetables into small pieces. Boil for 10–15 minutes until tender.
2. Meanwhile, cook the pasta until done.
3. Using an electric hand-held blender, purée most of the vegetables while still hot. Be careful not to splash yourself.
4. Add the vegetable broth cube, cumin powder and salt and pepper to taste.
5. Add the pasta.

Serve with pita bread.

Serves 5

2	stalks of celery	2
2	medium tomatoes	2
1	carrot	1
1	medium onion	1
¼	cabbage (shredded)	¼
1	bunch of English parsley	1
½ cup	alphabet pasta or elbow macaroni	120 mL
1	vegetable broth cube	1
½ tsp.	jeera (cumin powder)	2.5 mL
½ tsp.	salt	2.5 mL
½ tsp.	ground black pepper	2.5 mL

Chakri

2 cups	water	475 mL
1 tsp.	salt (or to taste)	5 mL
1 tsp.	sugar (or to taste)	5 mL
½ tsp.	haldi (turmeric)	2.5 mL
½ tsp.	chili powder	2.5 mL
1 Tbsp.	sesame seeds	15 mL
1 cup	sooji (cream of wheat)	240 mL
½ tsp.	salted butter	2.5 mL
2 cups	rice flour	475 mL

*E*ast Indians have their own version of a pasta machine for making noodles that are used to make a crispy snack called Chakri. Chakri can be stored in a container for at least 3 weeks, but I can assure you they will be finished in no time. I have discovered that serving Chakris with a Faluda drink (page 154) makes them irresistible!

1. Put the water, salt, sugar, turmeric and chili powder on to boil in a saucepan.
2. Add the sesame seeds when the water is boiling.
3. Add the cream of wheat and keep stirring until it becomes thick.
4. Turn onto a flat surface. Add the butter and knead while adding flour until it becomes like chapati dough (soft and pliable). Knead until there are no lumps.
5. Put in the chakri machine in batches. Pipe out the chakri and deep-fry on low heat.

Serves 10

 You can buy Chakri machines in most East Indian stores. Some are made of stainless steel, others are brass.

Methi na Dhebra

A wonderful Gujarati dish for Sunday brunches. This type of Roti is perfect for picnics when cut in quarters and served cold with raita or green chutney.

1. In a large dish, combine the fenugreek, yogurt, salt, turmeric, sugar, ginger and chopped chili. Marinate for 15 minutes.
2. Add the vegetable oil.
3. Gradually add the flour to make a soft and pliable dough.
4. Cover with a moist cloth, and let stand for 1 hour.
5. Form into small balls (about the size of golf balls) and roll out flat (almost the size of a saucer). This is now called dhebra.
6. Place each dhebra in a medium hot frying pan. Add ½ tsp. (2.5 mL) oil in drops around. Fry until golden brown on both sides, turning once.

Makes 10–12

2	bunches of methi (fenugreek) (chopped, leaves only)	2
1 ½ cups	yogurt	360 mL
½ tsp.	salt	2.5 mL
1 tsp.	haldi (turmeric)	5 mL
2 tsp.	sugar	10 mL
2 inch	piece ginger (chopped)	5 cm
1	green chili (chopped)	1
5 Tbsp.	vegetable oil	75 mL
5 cups	all-purpose flour	1.2 L
½ cup	vegetable oil	120 mL

 Methi is fenugreek leaves with the stems. The stems are usually very thick and cannot be eaten, so only the leaves are used.

Dhokra

A very famous and tasty Gujarati dish served on festive evenings. The best flavors are achieved by adding the chutney and vaghar just before serving. You may omit these and just serve it with chili sauce but you would lose the authentic Gujarati style.

Ingredients for dhokra:

2 cups	rice	475 mL
1 cup	channa daal (split chickpeas)	240 mL
1 cup	yogurt	240 mL
¼ tsp.	yeast	1.2 mL
3 cups	warm water	720 mL
2 (+ 1 Tbsp.)	green chilies	2 (+ 15 mL)
3 Tbsp.	cilantro (chopped)	45 mL
½ tsp.	garlic paste	2.5 mL
1 tsp.	salt	5 mL
½ tsp.	haldi (turmeric)	2.5 mL
2 Tbsp.	vegetable oil	30 mL
4 cups	water	950 mL
4 tsp.	Eno fruit salt (plain only)	20 mL

Method for dhokra:

1. Wash and soak the rice and channa daal in two separate bowls for 6–7 hours or overnight.
2. Drain and blend them together to make a batter with yogurt, yeast and warm water. The batter should be of the same consistency as pancake batter. Set it aside in a warm place to rise for 4–5 hours.
3. Blend together the 2 green chilies, 2 Tbsp. (30 mL) of the cilantro and the garlic paste and add to the above batter. Then add salt, turmeric, the remaining 1 Tbsp. (15 mL) of both chopped cilantro and green chilies, and 2 Tbsp. of oil to batter.
4. Heat about 4 cups (950 mL) of water in a large pot. Place a steamer on top to hold a heatproof plate.
5. When the water is boiling put about ¼ of the batter in a small bowl and add 1 tsp. (5 mL) Eno fruit salt. Mix until frothy and pour into a 9–10 inch (22.5–25 cm) diameter greased aluminum plate or tray. Place the tray in the steamer and cover with a tight-fitting lid. Steam for 7–8 minutes. Remove and let cool. Repeat the process 3 more times.

Method for vaghar:

1. Put oil in a frying pan on medium high heat. Add the mustard seeds, green chilies, coriander seeds, cumin and curry leaves. When the mustard seeds start popping up, add the coconut, lemon juice, turmeric, sugar, salt and chopped cilantro. Mix together and cook for 1 minute.

Method for chutney:

1. Heat vegetable oil on medium high in a small saucepan. Add crushed coriander seeds and garlic. Stir quickly and then add chili powder and tomato purée. If it is very thick then add a little lemon juice or water. Layer on top of the dhokra.

To serve, cut the dhokra in 10 diamond or square shapes and sprinkle with the vaghar and chutney mixture.

Serves 8

Ingredients for vaghar/tempering:

2 Tbsp.	oil	30 mL
1 tsp.	rai (black mustard seeds)	5 mL
4	green chilies	4
1 Tbsp.	coriander seeds (crushed)	15 mL
½ tsp.	jeera (cumin seeds)	2.5 mL
10	limro (curry leaves)	10
2 cups	desiccated coconut	475 mL
1 Tbsp.	fresh lemon juice	15 mL
½ tsp.	haldi (turmeric)	2.5 mL
1 Tbsp.	sugar	15 mL
1 tsp.	salt	15 mL
2 Tbsp.	cilantro (chopped)	30 mL

Ingredients for chutney:

2 Tbsp.	vegetable oil	30 mL
2 Tbsp.	dhania (coriander seeds) (crushed)	30 mL
1 Tbsp.	grated garlic	15 mL
2 Tbsp	red chili powder	30 mL
2 Tbsp.	tomato purée	30 mL
1 tsp.	fresh lemon juice or water	5 mL
1 tsp.	salt	5 mL

Spinach Kebabs

1	onion (finely chopped)	1
1 tsp.	garlic paste	5 mL
1 tsp.	ginger paste	5 mL
1	egg (beaten)	1
1 lb.	minced beef	455 g
1	bunch of spinach (finely chopped)	1
1 cup	breadcrumbs	240 mL
2 tsp.	salt	10 mL
1 tsp.	ground black pepper	5 mL
1	potato (boiled and peeled)	1
1 tsp.	green chilies (chopped)	5 mL
½	bunch of cilantro (chopped)	½
1 tsp.	sesame seeds	5 mL
2 cups	oil for shallow-frying	475 mL

A *tempting appetizer that will delight all.*

1. In a bowl, mix together the onion, garlic paste, ginger paste and egg.
2. Blend in the minced beef, spinach, breadcrumbs, salt and pepper. Let sit for 1 hour in a cool place.
3. Mash the potato and add to the mixture.
4. Add the green chilies, coriander leaves and sesame seeds.
5. Mix well and divide the mixture into 12–15 round patties and place on a floured tray.
6. Heat oil in a large frying pan. Fry the patties on medium heat until golden brown.

Serve with salad and chutney of your choice.

Serves 5

Clockwise from top: Puri (p. 109), Butter Chicken (p. 51), Samosas (p. 24),
Kasta Kachori (p. 7), Pakoras (p. 8) and Coconut Chutney (p. 90)

Top: Dahi Vada (p. 42), **middle:** Dhania Chutney (p. 91),
bottom: Kholapuri Baigan (p. 32)

Shami Kebab (p. 22) with Coconut Chutney (p. 90)
and Faluda Drink (p. 154)

Clockwise from top left: Sambaal Saag (p. 39), Palak Paneer (p. 36) and Idli (p. 9)

Vegetable Kebabs

Another masterpiece from vegetable Kofta artists like Hamida and me. A truly delightful snack for discerning guests.

1. Chop soaked channa daal in a food processor (or mincer) until it resembles breadcrumbs.
2. Add the frozen vegetables, grated carrot and onions, green chili, spices, cinnamon stick, potato, pepper and salt to the minced daal.
3. Mix well. If the mixture is too moist and does not form into balls, add a tablespoon or two of channa (gram flour) or maizena.
4. Form into table tennis-sized balls and deep-fry on medium high heat.
5. Drain on kitchen paper to absorb extra oil.

Serve hot with lemon slices or chutney.

Makes 15

¼ cup	channa daal (split chickpeas) (soaked overnight)	60 mL
1 cup	frozen mixed vegetables	240 mL
1	carrot (grated)	1
1	medium onion (grated)	1
1 Tbsp.	green onion (chopped)	15 mL
2 tsp.	green chili (pounded)	10 mL
2 tsp.	dhania (coriander seeds) (crushed)	10 mL
1 tsp.	jeera (cumin seeds) (crushed)	5 mL
1	small cinnamon stick (pounded)	1
1	large potato (boiled and chopped)	1
2 tsp.	black pepper (crushed)	10 mL
1 tsp.	salt	5 mL
3–4 cups	oil for deep-frying	750–950 mL
	channa (gram flour) or maizena, if needed	

Dahi Kebabs

A favorite Hyderabadi dish, mild and easy to digest.

1 cup	yogurt	240 mL
2 Tbsp.	gram flour	30 mL
1 tsp.	salt	5 mL
1 tsp.	chili powder	5 mL
2 Tbsp.	garam masala	30 mL
1 tsp.	ground black pepper	5 mL
1 lb.	minced meat	455 g
2 Tbsp.	ghee or oil	30 mL
2	large onions (sliced)	2
1 tsp.	garlic paste	5 mL
½ tsp.	chili powder (for gravy)	2.5 mL
½ tsp.	salt (for gravy)	2.5 mL
3 Tbsp.	milk	45 mL

1. In a large dish, mix together the yogurt, gram flour, salt, chili powder, half of the garam masala and the pepper. Mix in the minced meat. Add a little water and, with wet hands, divide the meat mixture into 12 equal parts. Flatten them to make kebabs of similar shape and size.
2. In a frying pan heat the ghee or oil to medium high and fry the kebabs, a few at a time, until they are a light golden color.
3. In the same pan, fry the sliced onions to golden brown. Grind using a food processor and set aside.
4. In the same pan put the garlic paste, chili powder, salt, fried ground onions and remaining garam masala. Stir and fry for one minute until gravy thickens.
5. Pour the gravy over the kebabs, then pour the milk over them.

Serve with an Indian bread of your choice
(see pages 105–120).

Serves 6

Donut Kebabs

These fried spicy patties make a very good snack. Donut Kebabs are quite filling when served with Raita (see page 95) and a green salad.

1. In a large saucepan, mix the meat with the ginger paste, salt, garlic paste, onions, daal and potatoes.
2. Cook, covered, over medium heat in 1 cup (240 mL) of water until water evaporates.
3. Let cool. Add the green chilies and blend in food processor until half shredded.
4. Add the remaining ingredients to the mixture and mix well.
5. Shape meat mixture into patties and fry over medium heat.

You can also serve this with Coconut Chutney (page 90).

Serves 6

2 lbs.	beef (medium-sized pieces)	900 g
1 tsp.	ginger paste	5 mL
2 tsp.	salt	10 mL
1 tsp.	garlic paste	5 mL
5	onions (chopped)	5
2 Tbsp.	channa daal (soaked overnight, drained and rinsed)	30 mL
5	medium potatoes (peeled and cut in small pieces)	5
1 cup	water	240 mL
5	green chilies	5
1 Tbsp.	mint leaves (chopped)	15 mL
2	eggs (beaten)	2
1 tsp.	ground black pepper	5 mL
1 Tbsp.	cilantro (chopped)	15 mL
1 tsp.	garam masala	5 mL

Shami Kebabs

2 lbs.	lamb or beef (cubed)	900 g
1 tsp.	ginger paste	5 mL
2 tsp.	salt	10 mL
1 tsp.	garlic paste	5 mL
5	onions (chopped)	5
2 Tbsp.	channa daal (soaked overnight, drained and rinsed)	30 mL
5	medium potatoes (peeled and cut into small pieces)	5
1 ½ cups	water	360 mL
5	green chilies	5
1 Tbsp.	mint leaves (chopped)	15 mL
1 tsp.	ground black pepper	5 mL
1 Tbsp.	cilantro	15 mL
1 tsp.	garam masala	5 mL
2	eggs (beaten)	2
½ cup	vegetable oil	120 mL

*S*hami Kebabs are a very traditional and popular appetizer. There are many variations but this is the one I prefer. It's also one of my mother's favorites. Experiment with serving different types of chutneys with it.

1. In a large pan, mix the meat with the ginger paste, salt, garlic paste, onions, daal, potatoes and 1 ½ cups (360 mL) of water.
2. Cook, covered, on medium heat until the water evaporates, about 10 minutes.
3. Let cool then add the green chilies. Blend in a food processor until half puréed.
4. Add the mint, the remaining seasonings and 1 egg to the mixture. Mix well.
5. Shape the meat into a mini-donut, dip the donut into remaining beaten egg, and shallow-fry in a frying pan on high heat.

Serve with Coconut Chutney (page 90).

Serves 6

Tandoori Masala Chicken

Also known as "the king of kebabs" this is one of India's most famous dishes. Tandoori Chicken is an Indian delicacy and the tastiest way to barbecue chicken. Whenever I make this at home, I double the quantity and freeze the leftovers. The frozen leftovers always taste better, as the spices have been absorbed into the pieces of chicken. The best flavor is achieved by using thighs and wings and a longer marinating time. Although there are many variations of this recipe, all follow the same basics. This version has been passed down in the family from my grandmother.

1. Skin, wash and clean chicken.
2. Apply mixture of chili powder, lemon juice, salt and tandoori powder to chicken. Set aside for about 1 hour.
3. While chicken is sitting, remove whey of yogurt by hanging in a muslin cloth over a bowl for 1 hour.
4. Mix red chili, salt, ginger paste, garlic paste, lemon juice and vegetable oil with the yogurt to make the marinade. Pour over chicken and refrigerate for 3–4 hours, covered.
5. Cook in preheated oven at 400°F (200°C) for 30 minutes.
6. Baste with butter and cook for another 5 minutes.
7. Sprinkle with chaat masala powder.

Serve with onion rings and lemon wedges.

Serves 4

Variation:

Omit the tandoori powder and use boneless chicken cubes of 1 ½ inches (3.8 cm) to make Chicken Tikka. You can even barbecue the spiced chicken cubes instead of baking them in an oven. Serve with salad and naan.

2 lbs.	chicken	900 g
1 tsp.	red chili powder	5 mL
1 Tbsp.	fresh lemon juice	15 mL
1 tsp.	salt	5 mL
2 Tbsp.	tandoori powder	30 mL

For the marinade:

1 ½ cups	yogurt, whey removed	360 mL
1 tsp.	red chili powder	5 mL
1 tsp.	salt	5 mL
1 tsp.	ginger paste	5 mL
1 tsp.	garlic paste	5 mL
2 Tbsp.	fresh lemon juice	30 mL
2 Tbsp.	vegetable oil	30 mL
1 Tbsp.	melted butter for basting	15 mL

For the garnish:

1	portion onion rings (slices of 1 small or ½ large raw onion)	1
1	lemon (cut into wedges)	1
	pinch of chaat masala	

 Chaat masala is a spice mix usually made with salt, pepper, cumin seeds, ground ginger and dried mango. It is available at East Indian grocery stores.

Samosas (Beef or Chicken)

½ lb.	beef (extra lean ground) or chicken breast (ground)	225 g
¼ tsp.	ginger (crushed)	1.2 mL
¼ tsp.	garlic (crushed)	1.2 mL
½ tsp.	salt	2.5 mL
½ tsp.	chili powder (or to taste)	2.5 mL
¼ tsp.	curry powder	1.2 mL
1 tsp.	fresh lemon juice	5 mL
¼ tsp.	garam masala	1.2 mL
1	large onion (finely chopped)	1
2 tsp.	cilantro (chopped)	10 mL
2 Tbsp.	all-purpose flour	30 mL
3 Tbsp.	water	45 mL
12	samosa wrappers	12
4 cups	vegetable oil for deep-frying	950 mL
1	lemon (cut into pieces)	1

 Samosa wrappers can be found in all East Indian grocery stores in the freezer section.

"*Samosa wrappers,*" *more commonly known as* "*Samosa Par,*" *are found in ready-made packages in East Indian stores. They make an excellent snack for traveling or picnics, and can be spiced up quite easily by adding more chili powder. Samosas are much like Bhajiyas and Pakoras in the sense that, when served alongside any chutney, I guarantee there will be none left over. The recipe is extremely easy. The only difficult part is wrapping the triangular pocket.*

1. In a large saucepan, add the meat, ginger, garlic, salt, chili powder, curry powder and lemon juice.
2. Cook meat over medium heat stirring constantly and breaking up any lumps until all the liquid has evaporated and the meat almost sticks to the pan.
3. Remove pan from heat and add the garam masala, onion and chopped cilantro. Mix thoroughly.
4. Make a paste with the flour and water.
5. Put the meat mixture onto a samosa wrapper and fold into a pocket (see next page).
6. Touch up the corners with the paste so it does not open when deep-frying.

Serve garnished with lemon pieces.

Makes 12

How to stuff a Samosa

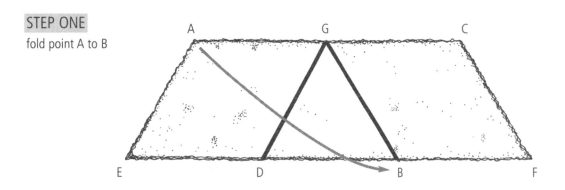

STEP ONE

fold point A to B

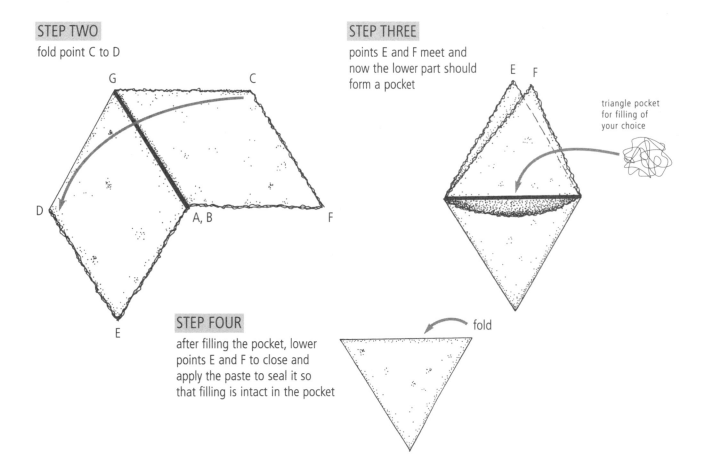

STEP TWO

fold point C to D

STEP THREE

points E and F meet and
now the lower part should
form a pocket

triangle pocket
for filling of
your choice

STEP FOUR

after filling the pocket, lower
points E and F to close and
apply the paste to seal it so
that filling is intact in the pocket

fold

Vegetable Samosas

3 cups	frozen hash browns	720 mL
1/2 cup	frozen peas	120 mL
3 Tbsp.	vegetable oil	45 mL
1/4 tsp.	rai (black mustard seeds)	1.2 mL
4	limro (curry leaves)	4
1/4 tsp.	jeera (cumin seeds)	1.2 mL
1/4 tsp.	dhania (coriander seeds) (crushed)	1.2 mL
1/4 tsp.	garlic (crushed)	1.2 mL
1/4 tsp.	haldi (turmeric)	1.2 mL
1/4 tsp.	chili powder	1.2 mL
1 tsp.	salt	5 mL
1 Tbsp.	fresh lemon juice	15 mL
1	large onion (finely chopped)	1
2 tsp.	cilantro (chopped)	10 mL
1/4 tsp.	garam masala	1.2 mL
2 Tbsp.	all-purpose flour	30 mL
3 Tbsp.	water	45 mL
15	samosa wrappers	15
4 cups	vegetable oil for deep-frying	950 mL
1	lemon (cut into pieces)	1

These are one of East India's most famous snacks. Samosas are a hit at any party or event and are guaranteed to make it into anyone's book of favorite recipes. The beauty of Vegetable Samosas is that they are not quite as oily as the meat ones and they are just as, if not more, delicious.

1. Microwave the hash browns and peas on high for 7 minutes.
2. In a pan heat oil to medium hot and then add the mustard seeds and curry leaves. Cook until mustard seeds crackle.
3. Add the cumin seeds, coriander seeds, garlic, turmeric, chili powder, salt and lemon juice.
4. Now add the hash browns and peas to the above mixture and mix thoroughly for 1 minute. Remove from heat.
5. Add the chopped onion, cilantro and garam masala.
6. Prepare a paste by mixing together the flour and water.
7. Put the vegetable mixture onto a samosa wrapper and fold into a pocket (see previous page). Touch up the corners with the paste so the samosa does not open when deep-frying.
8. Deep-fry in medium hot oil until golden brown.

Serve garnished with lemon pieces.

Makes 12–15

Vegetarian Curries and Side Dishes

In Indian cooking, vegetables are rarely boiled. They are more usually steamed, braised, curried or fried in their own natural juices, or sometimes with fresh lemon juice, curds or tomatoes.

Early East Indian immigrants introduced new varieties of vegetables to their new homeland. Many either brought seeds with them or later imported them and, with much tender nursing, we now have a fine selection of Indian vegetables growing on our farms. Bitter gourds, the different bhajis (spinaches), brinjals (eggplants), sprouted moong and bhinda (okra) are now more easily available.

East Indian cooks experiment constantly with vegetables. You can choose from the more simple curries to the Moghlai dishes, like Moghlai Spinach Saag (page 34), or the more unusual side dishes like Kholapuri Baigan (page 32). Moghlai cooking was introduced by the royal chefs of the Moghuls of India. It is no wonder then that East Indian vegetarian cookery is so rich and varied and that it is satisfying to both those who eat in order to exist and those who exist in order to eat.

Aloo Gobi (Potato Cauliflower Curry)

1	small cauliflower	1
4	large potatoes	4
1	medium onion	1
2–3	tomatoes	2–3
2 Tbsp.	fresh lemon juice	30 mL
2 Tbsp.	vegetable oil	30 mL
¼ tsp.	asafoetida	1.2 mL
½ tsp.	salt	2.5 mL
½ tsp.	haldi (turmeric)	2.5 mL
½ tsp.	dhania (coriander) (coarsely ground)	2.5 mL
1 tsp.	jeera (cumin) (coarsely ground)	5 mL
1 tsp.	chili powder	5 mL
1 tsp.	garam masala	5 mL

This curry can also be made with a combination of spinach and potato, cabbage and potato, peas and potato, or green beans and potato. Thanks to Meera for this one.

1. Separate cauliflower into small florets.
2. Peel and cut potatoes into small pieces.
3. Chop the onion and tomatoes, put into a bowl, and cover with the lemon juice.
4. In a saucepan, heat the vegetable oil to medium high and sauté the onions and tomatoes. Add the potatoes and fry for 10 minutes. Stir occasionally.
5. Add the cauliflower and fry for 3 minutes, stirring occasionally.
6. Collect all the dry spices, except the garam masala, in a bowl and add to the saucepan. The potatoes and cauliflower cook in their own moisture, so it is not necessary to add water.
7. When the potatoes are fully cooked (about 10 minutes), sprinkle with garam masala.

Serve with raita and chapatis.

Serves 4

Potato Curry

If you are a tomato lover, you will definitely enjoy this tangy potato dish. I would also recommend trying this with a daal dish and plain boiled rice! This is a quick low-fat recipe.

1. Boil the potatoes, peel them, and cut them into large cubes. Set aside.
2. Heat oil to medium hot in a pan, add mustard seeds and let them crack.
3. Add crushed tomatoes, cover and cook for 4 minutes. Then stir in curry powder.
4. Add chili powder and paprika, and reduce heat.
5. Add salt and sugar to the potatoes and then add them to the sauce. Cook for 5 minutes.

Serve with parathas or a colorful rice pilau.

Serves 4

6–7	medium potatoes	6–7
½ tsp.	rai (black mustard seeds)	2.5 mL
1 cup	crushed tomatoes	240 mL
1 ½ tsp.	curry powder	7.5 mL
1 tsp.	chili powder	5 mL
2 tsp.	paprika	10 mL
½ tsp.	salt (or to taste)	2.5 mL
2 ½ tsp.	sugar	12.5 mL

Bhinda Curry (Okra Curry)

1 lb.	bhinda (okra)	455 g
¼ cup	vegetable oil	60 mL
2	medium onions	2
¾ cup	tomato (finely chopped)	180 mL
1 tsp.	chili powder	5 mL
1 tsp.	curry powder	5 mL
½ tsp.	ginger (crushed)	2.5 mL
½ tsp.	garlic (crushed)	2.5 mL
1 tsp.	haldi (turmeric)	5 mL
2 tbsp.	yogurt	30 mL
½ tsp.	garam masala	2.5 mL

Bhinda, the Indian name for okra, is the star ingredient in this tangy vegetable dish that can be served on almost any occasion. Personalizing this curry by varying the amount of chilies added will in no way lessen the flavor. Bhinda is perfect as a side dish or main dish, but my favorite is to serve it on a bed of lettuce and chapatis with a variety of Indian salads.

1. Wash the okra. Dry well on a cloth. Remove the head and tail portion and cut into lengths of half an inch (1.2 cm).
2. Deep-fry in the oil until light brown then remove from the oil. The frying seals the okra.
3. Slice the onions and fry on medium high heat until pale golden brown.
4. Add the tomatoes and all the spices, except the garam masala, and cook for 5 minutes until the curry has blended nicely.
5. Add the fried okra and cook for approximately 5 minutes, then add the yogurt.
6. Add the garam masala just before serving and mix well.

Serves 4

Green Pepper Curry

A blend of rich aromatic spices, this vegetarian dish will provide a delightful alternative to your everyday diet. Although Green Pepper Curry is normally served as a main dish, it can be served alongside chicken or mutton curry to give excellent variety. Using a red onion in place of the white one will further enhance the rich flavor. This recipe is sure to be a favorite with those who like their food hot and spicy!

1. Wash the green peppers in cold water to retain crispness.
2. Slice the peppers vertically in half, ensuring the stalk remains attached. Set aside.
3. Roast the sesame seeds, coriander seeds, poppy seeds, cumin seeds, peanuts and desiccated coconut lightly in the oven at 325°F (160°C), being careful not to brown them. This should take approximately 5–6 minutes.
4. Using a mortar and pestle or a rolling pin, coarsely crush the spices. Set aside.
5. Fry the onion in the oil on medium high heat until almost light brown in color.
6. Toss in the coarsely ground spices and fry for 1 minute. Add the crushed garlic.
7. Stuff some of this mixture into the green peppers, and pour the rest over all the peppers.
8. Dilute the tamarind paste with 3–4 Tbsp. (45–60 mL) of water and pour over the spiced peppers.
9. Cook for 10 minutes on top of the stove on low heat.

Serve with salad and bhaturas or chapatis.

Serves 4

½ lb.	long green peppers, mild (approximately 8)	225 g
2 Tbsp.	sesame seeds	30 mL
1 Tbsp.	whole dhania (coriander seeds)	15 mL
2 Tbsp.	khus khus (poppy seeds)	30 mL
1 Tbsp.	jeera (cumin seeds)	15 mL
1 Tbsp.	peanuts	15 mL
2 Tbsp.	desiccated coconut	30 mL
1	medium onion (grated)	1
2 tsp.	garlic (crushed)	10 mL
2 Tbsp.	vegetable oil	30 mL
2 Tbsp.	tamarind paste, diluted	30 mL

Kholapuri Baigan

4	medium bringals (eggplants)	4
1 tsp.	salt	5 mL
1 cup	vegetable oil for deep-frying	240 mL
2 1/4 cups	yogurt	535 mL
1/2 tsp.	jeera (cumin)	2.5 mL
1/4 tsp.	garlic paste	1.2 mL
1 Tbsp.	mint leaves (chopped)	15 mL
1	small English cucumber (optional)	1
1 tsp.	chaat masala (see page 23)	5 mL
2	medium potatoes (boiled)	2
1 tsp.	cilantro (chopped)	5 mL
1 tsp.	chaat masala (for garnishing)	5 mL
2 Tbsp.	vegetable oil	30 mL
1/2 tsp.	rai (black mustard seeds)	2.5 mL
1/2 tsp.	jeera (cumin)	2.5 mL

Even though my son, Zuher, simply despises eggplants, he really enjoys this dish. This is one of those recipes that can be prepared a day in advance. If you are not an eggplant lover or if you know someone who does not enjoy them, try this dish.

1. Cut eggplants into rings 1/4 inch (.6 cm) thick and salt them. Set aside for 10 minutes.
2. Using paper towel, pat them dry then deep-fry in a cast-iron pan until both sides are golden brown. Once done, place on clean paper towel to remove any excess oil.
3. Prepare the yogurt mixture as you would do for Raita (see page 95), using the cumin, garlic paste, chopped mint leaves, cucumber (if using) and chaat masala.
4. Cut the boiled potatoes into small cubes and put them in a glass dish (preferably oval). Place the eggplants on top of the potatoes.
5. Pour the yogurt mixture evenly over the eggplant. The dish can be prepared ahead of time to this point.
6. Prior to serving, heat 2 Tbsp. (30 mL) oil in a cast-iron pan. Add the mustard seeds and cumin. When they begin to pop, pour immediately over the yogurt mixture.

Serve with rice or bhaturas.

Serves 5

Nariyal Mohogo (Cassava with Coconut)

Mohogo, or cassava, is like a potato and is found in Indian and Filipino grocery stores. To turn this recipe into a complete meal, stir in some pieces of boiled mutton after it has been cooked.

4	large mohogo (cassava)	4
4 cups	water	950 mL
1 tsp.	salt	5 mL
½ tsp.	chili powder	2.5 mL
1 ⅔ cups	coconut milk	400 mL

1. Boil mohogo in 4 cups (950 mL) of water. Make sure the mohogo is not bitter (by tasting it after boiling).
2. Set aside and when cool cut lengthwise into slices about 3 inches (7.5 cm) long.
3. Add salt and chili powder to the mohogo.
4. Spoon the coconut milk into three parts: very thick, slightly thick and thin.
5. In a saucepan pour the thin milk over the mohogo and cook until it comes to a slow boil.
6. Pour over the slightly thick milk. Bring to a slight boil.
7. Pour over the thick milk and bring to boil.

Serve with lemon slices and Coconut Chutney (page 90).

Serves 4

Moghlai Spinach Saag
(Spinach Cooked Kashmiri Style)

1 lb.	spinach (washed)	455 g
2 Tbsp.	mustard oil	30 mL
½ tsp.	jeera (cumin seeds)	2.5 mL
1 tsp.	dried methi (dried fenugreek leaves)	5 mL
1 tsp.	crushed ginger	1.2 mL
½ tsp.	haldi (ground turmeric)	2.5 mL
½ tsp.	ground fennel	2.5 mL
2	fresh green chilies (seeded and sliced)	2
1 tsp.	salt (or to taste)	5 mL
½ cup	peas (fresh or frozen)	120 mL

Optional ingredients:

¼ tsp.	powdered asafoetida	1.2 mL
1 cup	potato (peeled, diced)	240 mL
½ cup	cashews	120 mL

In India there are many varieties of spinach, some of which can be found in North America in Indian or even Chinese grocery stores. But you can also use the spinach available in your domestic grocery stores. Most Rajasthani people have this dish with Moghlai naans (found in Indian grocery stores). I prepare this dish on traditional days like the Eid festival or during the festive days in the month of Rajab, as it is my family's favorite dish.

1. Put the washed spinach in a colander to drain. Chop the leaves up and discard the stems.
2. Heat the oil in a saucepan to medium high and add asafoetida (if using), cumin seeds, fenugreek leaves and ginger.
3. Fry for 1 minute, stirring.
4. Add the remaining ingredients and the optional ingredients if using and fry for 1 minute. Now add the spinach and stir well.
5. Cover and cook until the potatoes are soft, about 10 minutes.
6. Add a little water if necessary.

Serve with Masala Bhaath (page 130).

Serves 4

Mustard oil can be found in East Indian grocery stores.

Simply Indian

Paneer

ada Paneer is a brand of solid milk cheese sold in East Indian stores in the freezer section. Here is how you can make your own.

1. Boil the milk.
2. Add the yogurt and salt. Reduce the heat and stir well for 15 minutes.
3. Let set for 20 minutes. This will curdle the milk.
4. Take a muslin cloth and pour the curdled milk into it. Place this into a sieve and tie the cloth up. Leave it for a few hours.
5. Put weights on it and leave overnight. It will form into a cheese that can be cut into cubes.

4 1/4 cups	milk (homogenized)	1 L
2 cups	yogurt	475 mL
2 1/2 tsp.	salt	12.5 mL

Palak Paneer (Spinach with Paneer)

3	large bunches of spinach	3
4 Tbsp.	vegetable oil	60 mL
6	methi seeds (fenugreek)	6
½ tsp.	jeera (cumin seeds)	2.5 mL
¼ tsp.	kasuri methi (dried methi leaves)	1.2 mL
¼ tsp.	haldi (turmeric)	1.2 mL
2	large tomatoes (chopped)	2
¼ tsp.	garlic (crushed)	1.2 mL
¼ tsp.	ginger (crushed)	1.2 mL
2 Tbsp.	fried onions (sliced)	30 mL
1	green chili	1
2 cups	whipping cream	475 mL
2 cups	paneer (either half package or homemade— see page 35)	475 mL

This dish is reserved for important occasions and with its wonderful assortment of spices it is truly fit for royalty. Palak means spinach and paneer is Indian cheese, very similar to feta cheese. Paneer can be found in most Indian grocery stores or tofu could be used as a substitute. Many cooks in India have subtle variations of this dish.

1. Chop spinach finely and leave to soak in water to dislodge any soil particles.
2. Heat the vegetable oil in a pot on medium high heat.
3. Add the methi seeds, cumin, methi leaves and turmeric and cook for 1 minute.
4. Add the tomatoes, garlic and ginger. Cook for another 3 minutes.
5. Squeeze excess water from the spinach and add to the pot with the fried onions.
6. Cook until the spinach is almost sticking to the pan.
7. When the water is almost gone, transfer the ingredients to a blender. Add a little bit of water and blend.
8. Return to the pot, add the whipping cream and bring to a boil. Remove from heat.
9. Add half package of Dada Paneer or 2 cups (475 mL) homemade paneer to the cooked spinach.

Serve hot.

Serves 4

Spinach Curry with Beans and Coconut

*T*his is a very common dish amongst East Indian families living in East Africa.

1. Chop spinach finely, leave to soak in water to dislodge any soil particles then drain well, removing as much water as possible.
2. Heat vegetable oil on medium high in a large pot. Add the onion to the oil and sauté.
3. Add the drained spinach to the sautéed onions. Cook until all the water has evaporated and the spinach starts to stick to the pot.
4. Add salt, garlic paste, green chili chutney (see below) and beans.
5. Cook for 2 minutes and then add the coconut milk.
6. Cook for 3–5 minutes and then remove from heat.

Serve with either rice or chapatis.

Serves 5

3	bunches of spinach	3
4 Tbsp.	vegetable oil	60 mL
1	onion (finely chopped)	1
½ tsp.	salt	2.5 mL
½ tsp.	garlic paste	2.5 mL
1	green chili (chopped)	1
½ cup	black-eyed beans (soaked overnight and boiled for approximately 15–20 minutes)	120 mL
1 cup	coconut milk	240 mL
½ tsp.	green chili chutney	2.5 mL

Green chili chutney:

6	green chilies	6
½ tsp.	jeera (cumin)	2.5 mL
1	large clove garlic	1
1 Tbsp.	fresh lemon juice	15 mL
¼ tsp.	salt	1.2 mL

Mix together in a blender until completely liquid. Refrigerate in a glass jar for up to one week.

Mixed Vegetable Curry

For a more beautiful dish, slice the vegetables diagonally.

1	eggplant	1
2	medium potatoes	2
1	medium onion	1
3	medium carrots	3
1	medium cauliflower	1
6 Tbsp.	vegetable oil	90 mL
4	methi seeds (fenugreek seeds)	4
1/4 tsp.	rai (black mustard seeds)	1.2 mL
2	medium tomatoes	2
1/2 tsp.	garlic (crushed)	2.5 mL
1/2 tsp.	ginger (crushed)	2.5 mL
1/2 tsp.	salt	2.5 mL
1/2 tsp.	chili powder	2.5 mL
1/2 tsp.	haldi (turmeric)	2.5 mL
1/2 tsp.	ground jeera (cumin seeds)	2.5 mL
1 tsp.	khatai (dried mango powder)	5 mL
	cilantro (for garnish)	

Mango powder, also known as khatai, is available in all East Indian grocery stores.

1. Wash the eggplant, and cut into slices 2 inches (5 cm) thick. Salt the slices.
2. Peel the potatoes and cut into similar sized pieces as the eggplant. Do the same for the onion and carrots.
3. Wash and cut up the cauliflower into 1-inch (2.5-cm) pieces.
4. Heat the oil to medium high and fry the eggplant pieces until they become golden brown. Remove from the heat and set aside.
5. Reheat same oil to medium high and add the fenugreek seeds and mustard seeds. Cook until they start to pop and release their aroma.
6. Add the onions, chopped tomatoes and other vegetables. Cook for approximately 10 minutes until the vegetables are tender.
7. Now add the rest of the spices except the mango powder.
8. Cook on low heat until the vegetables are completely cooked.
9. Add a little water if necessary and add the mango powder and cilantro for garnish.

Serve with chapatis or puris.

Serves 5

Helpful Hint:
Cutting up the potatoes and carrots and microwaving them in a bowl of water on high will speed up the cooking process. You can then add this to the tomatoes in step 6.

Sambaal Saag

*S*plit beans and lentils are called daal. This authentic daal dish is very common in southern India and is especially popular with vegetarians. Preparing the sambaal powder fresh complements the flavor of this spicy dish as it retains the full rich aroma and taste of exotic Indian spices. Southern chefs have produced a plethora of vegetarian delights to supplement their various daal and rice dishes.

Method for sambaal powder:
1. Take all the ingredients except the chili powder and dry roast in a frying pan on medium high heat.
2. Let cool for 10 minutes then blend the ingredients in a coffee grinder.
3. Add the chili powder.

Method for daal curry:
1. Put the daal to cook in 2 cups (475 mL) of water, and add the oil and turmeric. Cook for 15 minutes on medium high heat.
2. Microwave the frozen vegetables on high for 7 minutes. Set aside.
3. Once the daal is cooked and mushy, whisk lightly, and add the vegetables.
4. In a food processor or blender, blend the fresh grated coconut with the crushed garlic, sambaal powder and ½ cup (120 mL) water.
5. Add this to the daal and vegetables and mix thoroughly, bringing it to a boil. This is daal curry.
6. While this cooks, heat 2 Tbsp. (30 mL) of oil in a pan and add the mustard seeds, curry leaves and chopped cilantro. Pour over the daal curry.
7. Add the freshly squeezed lemon juice and salt to taste.

Serve with Idlis (see page 9).

Serves 4

Ingredients for sambaal powder:

¼ tsp.	rai (black mustard seeds)	1.2 mL
¼ tsp.	methi (fenugreek seeds)	1.2 mL
¼ tsp.	jeera (cumin seeds)	1.2 mL
¼ tsp.	saunf (fennel seeds)	1.2 mL
¼ tsp.	chili powder	1.2 mL

Ingredients for daal curry::

2 Tbsp.	sambaal powder	30 mL
1 cup	toor daal (split pigeon peas)	240 mL
2 cups	water	475 mL
1 Tbsp.	vegetable oil	15 mL
1 tsp.	haldi (turmeric)	5 mL
½ cup	frozen vegetables	120 mL
¼ cup	fresh grated coconut	60 mL
¼ tsp.	garlic (crushed)	1.2 mL
½ cup	water	120 mL
2 Tbsp.	vegetable oil	30 mL
½ tsp.	rai (black mustard seeds)	2.5 mL
3–4	limro (curry leaves)	3–4
1	bunch of cilantro	1
2	fresh lemons (squeezed)	2
	salt to taste	

Daal Curry

2 cups	orange daal (lentils)	475 mL
¼ tsp.	haldi (turmeric)	1.2 mL
4 Tbsp.	vegetable oil	60 mL
1 tsp.	rai (black mustard seeds)	5 mL
6	limro (curry leaves)	6
2	medium tomatoes (chopped)	2
3 Tbsp.	fried onions	45 mL
1 tsp.	crushed garlic	5 mL
½ tsp.	kasuri methi (methi leaves)	2.5 mL
1 tsp.	curry powder	5 mL
½ tsp.	salt	2.5 mL
½ tsp.	chili powder	2.5 mL
2 tsp.	sugar	10 mL
1 cup	water	240 mL
½ tsp.	garam masala	2.5 mL
1	bunch of cilantro (chopped)	1

No vegetarian meal is complete without a daal.

1. Wash lentils. In a large saucepan with plenty of water, bring to a boil with turmeric and cook until overdone and mushy, approximately 15 minutes.
2. In a different saucepan, heat the oil on medium heat. Add the mustard seeds and curry leaves until the seeds start to pop (no more than 30 seconds).
3. Add the tomatoes and fry for about 3 minutes. Add onions, garlic, methi leaves, curry powder, salt, chili powder and sugar.
4. Add the mashed lentils and boil for 5 minutes. Add 1 cup (240 mL) of water to dilute the curry consistency.
5. Remove from heat and add garam masala.
6. Sprinkle with chopped cilantro before serving.

Serve with chapatis or rice.

Serves 4

Channa Daal Curry

*C*hanna, one of India's many indigenous lentils, is widely used in Gujarati cooking. The beauty of the Channa Daal Curry is that it needs only simple garnishes to be a very tasty meal. My friend Bindu and I enjoy our Channa Daal Curry with a tangy slice of lemon, savory rice and a side serving of Carrot Pickles (see page 96). However, it can also be served with chapatis, or as a hot soup on icy cold nights. On special occasions, it makes an excellent accompaniment for other vegetarian dishes.

1. Boil the daal in about 3 ½ cups (840 mL) water in a medium-sized pot, half covered, for approximately 20 minutes.
2. In a deep frying pan, heat the oil on medium high.
3. Fry the onion until it is almost golden to light brown, then add the tomato.
4. Add the turmeric, garlic paste, chili powder, salt and asafoetida and fry for 5 minutes.
5. Add the tomato purée and the boiled daal.
6. Cook for about 5 minutes, then add 2 cups (475 mL) of water. Bring the whole mixture to a boil.
7. Add the potatoes, garam masala and khatai powder. Cook the curry for another 5–10 minutes.
8. Sprinkle with chopped cilantro before serving.

Serves 6

2 cups	channa daal (soaked overnight)	475 mL
3 ½ cups	water	840 mL
5 Tbsp.	vegetable oil	75 mL
1	medium onion (chopped)	1
1	medium tomato (chopped)	1
½ tsp.	haldi (turmeric powder)	2.5 mL
½ tsp.	garlic paste	2.5 mL
1 tsp.	chili powder	5 mL
1 tsp.	salt	5 mL
¼ tsp.	asafoetida powder	1.2 mL
2 tsp.	tomato purée	10 mL
2 cups	water	475 mL
2	medium potatoes (boiled and diced)	2
½ tsp.	garam masala	2.5 mL
½ tsp.	khatai (dried mango powder)	2.5 mL
1	small sprig cilantro (chopped)	1

Channa is chickpeas whereas Channa Daal is split chickpeas.

Dahi Vada

2 cups	urad daal	475 mL
½ cup	water	120 mL
1 tsp.	salt	5 mL
1 tsp.	chili powder	5 mL
4 Tbsp.	vegetable oil	60 mL
2 cups	yogurt	475 mL
1 tsp.	sugar	5 mL
4 Tbsp.	chaat masala (see page 23)	60 mL
	salt to taste	
5 Tbsp.	tamarind sauce	75 mL
	chili powder (for garnish)	

Urad daal is split mah beans and can be found at your local supermarket.

*O*riginally a Gujarati dish, Dahi Vada is now made all over India and is popular in all Indian restaurants.

1. Soak the daal overnight. Drain, rinse and blend gently in a blender with about ½ cup (120 mL) water the next day.
2. Add the salt and chili powder and leave for 5–6 hours or overnight.
3. Form into small patties the next day and fry in hot oil, 6–7 patties at a time.
4. Fry until golden brown then drain on a wire basket, allowing the excess oil to drain onto a plate below.
5. Soak the patties in a bowl of lukewarm salted water. Squeeze the patties gently between the palms of your hands to remove excess water.
6. Put into a casserole dish.
7. Mix the yogurt with the sugar, ¼ tsp. (1.2 mL) of the chaat masala and a little bit of salt to taste.
8. If the mixture is very thick, add a little water.
9. Pour over the patties, sprinkle with the remaining chaat masala, tamarind sauce and chili powder.

Decorate with a few sprigs of cilantro before serving.

Serves 4

Masoor Daal Curry

Masoor daal (red lentils) is the quickest type of daal to cook. It can also be used without previous soaking if one is in a hurry. In general, the dried beans should be rehydrated for an hour or so to shorten the cooking time. This dish can be made in advance and refrigerated up to two days, or frozen up to two weeks. I had never really noticed this smooth-tasting curry until I tried this recipe at my cousin Nusrat's house. Accompanied with rice and chapatis, it has become one of my favorite dishes.

2 cups	masoor daal (red lentils)	475 mL
3 cups	water	720 mL
1/4 tsp.	haldi (turmeric powder)	1.2 mL
4 Tbsp.	vegetable oil	60 mL
1 tsp.	rai (black mustard seeds)	5 mL
6	limro (curry leaves)	6
2	tomatoes (chopped)	2
2 Tbsp.	fried onions	30 mL
1 tsp.	curry powder	5 mL
1 tsp.	garlic (crushed)	5 mL
1/2 tsp.	salt	2.5 ml
1/2 tsp.	chili powder	2.5 mL
1 Tbsp.	chopped cilantro	15 mL
2	lemons (squeezed)	2
1/2 tsp.	garam masala	2.5 mL
2 Tbsp.	chopped cilantro (for garnish)	30 mL

1. Wash the masoor daal. In a pot add the water, daal, turmeric powder and 1 Tbsp. (15 mL) of the oil. Boil for approximately 20 minutes, or until cooked. When ready, the lentils will be almost mushy.
2. Heat the remaining 3 Tbsp. (45 mL) oil in another pot to a medium heat. Add the mustard seeds and curry leaves. Fry until the seeds start to pop.
3. Add the chopped tomatoes. Fry for 1 minute, then add the onions, curry powder, crushed garlic, salt and chili powder.
4. Mash the daal slightly with a potato masher and add to the above mixture. Let cook for at least 5 minutes. If the daal consistency is very thick you can add water to make it thinner (1 1/2 cups/360 mL water).
5. Add the cilantro, the freshly squeezed lemon juice and garam masala. Let simmer for about 4 minutes and remove from the heat.
7. Sprinkle with chopped cilantro before serving.

Serve with rice or chapatis.

Serves 6

Mung Bean Curry

2 cups	mung beans (sorted, washed and soaked overnight)	475 mL
6 cups	water	1.5 L
1 tsp.	salt	5 mL
4 Tbsp.	vegetable oil	60 mL
1	large onion (chopped)	1
2	medium tomatoes (chopped)	2
1 tsp.	garlic (crushed)	5 mL
1 tsp.	ginger (crushed)	5 mL
1 tsp.	dhania (ground coriander)	5 mL
1 tsp.	jeera (ground cumin)	5 mL
½ tsp.	red chili powder (or to taste)	2.5 mL
¼ tsp.	haldi (turmeric)	1.25 mL
1 ½ tsp.	tomato paste	7.5 mL
½ tsp.	salt (or to taste)	2.5 mL
¼ tsp.	garam masala	1.25 mL
1 Tbsp.	fresh lemon juice	15 mL
1 Tbsp.	cilantro (chopped)	15 mL

Some people like this curry to have a thin consistency but I do not. The beauty of the preparation is that it remains thick and all the mung daal seeds separate.

1. Put the mung beans in a large saucepan with the water and salt. Bring to a boil. Lower heat and cook for 30 minutes or until tender. Drain the water, saving about ½ cup (120 mL).
2. In another saucepan heat the oil and add the onion. Sauté until golden brown. Add the tomatoes, garlic, ginger, coriander, cumin, chili powder, turmeric, tomato paste and salt.
3. Add the mung beans and reserved liquid to this, reduce the heat and let simmer for 20 minutes. If curry becomes too dry, add water.
4. Add lemon juice.
5. Garnish with chopped cilantro.

Serve with rice or chapatis.

Serves 5

Uppuma

A famous south Indian dish usually served for breakfast. Uppuma at my place has become a traditional weekend breakfast.

1. Heat oil in a wok, and add the black mustard seeds and curry leaves to it. Then add the channa daal.
2. Fry until the daal turns brown, then add the onion and sauté for a few minutes.
3. Add the green chili, chili powder, garlic paste and turmeric powder.
4. Add the cashew nuts, salt and 2 ½ cups (600 mL) of water.
5. When water is really boiling, start sprinkling in the cream of wheat. Mix well.
6. Cover and keep on low heat for 10–15 minutes.

Serve with parathas, chapatis or alone.

Serves 4–5

3 Tbsp.	vegetable oil	45 mL
1 tsp.	rai (black mustard seeds)	5 mL
8	limro (curry leaves)	8
1 Tbsp.	channa daal (washed)	15 mL
1	onion	1
1	green chili (chopped)	1
½ tsp.	chili powder	2.5 mL
1 tsp.	garlic paste	5 mL
1 tsp.	haldi (turmeric powder)	5 mL
¼ cup	cashew nuts (chopped)	60 mL
½ tsp.	salt	2.5 mL
2 ½ cups	water	600 mL
1 ½ cups	sooji (cream of wheat)	360 mL

My top tip for working with hot peppers? I dip my fingers in oil prior to cutting green chilies or any hot peppers to protect my fingers from burning.

Masala Dosa (Indian Pancakes)

Ingredients for dosa (batter):

1 cup	rice	240 mL
1/2 cup	urad daal	120 mL
8	methi seeds (fenugreek)	8
1/2 tsp	salt	2.5 mL
1 Tbsp.	vegetable oil	15 mL

Ingredients for potato filling:

1 Tbsp.	vegetable oil	15 mL
1/2 tsp.	rai (black mustard seeds)	2.5 mL
1/2 tsp	haldi (turmeric)	2.5 mL
1	medium onion (chopped)	1
3	green chilies	3
1 inch	piece ginger (chopped)	2.5 cm
2 Tbsp.	fresh lemon juice	30 mL
3 cups	frozen hash browns (defrosted)	720 mL
	salt to taste	

Masala Dosa consists of the two main ingredients, rice and daal, that form the heart and soul of southern Indian vegetarian meals. Preparation for this dish takes two days. Masala Dosa can be served as dinner, breakfast or snack.

1. In separate bowls, soak the rice, urad daal and fenugreek seeds overnight.

Day 1

2. The next day, drain and blend each into a fine smooth paste in a blender using a little water, then mix them together.
3. Add salt to taste and place the batter in a plastic container in the fridge to ferment for one day. (The oil will be used for frying on Day 2.)
4. Prepare the potato filling. Heat the vegetable oil in a frying pan on medium high heat and add the mustard seeds, turmeric, onion, green chilies, ginger and lemon juice.
5. Microwave the hash browns for 4 minutes, add to the frying pan, mix well and add salt to taste.
6. Prepare the channa chutney. Roast the channa daal dry in a frying pan on medium high heat, stirring continuously until red in color.
7. Add the rest of the ingredients and mix in a blender to form a nice smooth paste.

Day 2

8. On the second day, using a large non-stick frying pan, heat oil on a medium low heat, and spread a ladle full of batter evenly on it. This has to be done quickly.

9 Cover with a lid and cook like a pancake for approximately 1 minute. The steam will cook it evenly inside.

10. When bubbly, spread 1 ½ tsp. (7.5 mL) of channa chutney evenly on the pancake.

11. Now add 1 ½ Tbsp. (22.5 mL) of potato filling, fold the pancake in half and serve hot.

12. Repeat the same process until all the batter is used.

Makes 8

Ingredients for channa chutney:

1 ½ cups	channa daal	360 mL
1 Tbsp.	vegetable oil	15 mL
1	large onion (chopped)	1
½ tsp.	chili powder	2.5 mL
5 Tbsp.	tamarind sauce	75 mL
¼ tsp.	asafoetida	2.5 mL
1	bunch of mint leaves	1
1 cup	water	240 mL
½ tsp.	salt	2.5 mL

Punjabi Chole

1 cup	fresh kabuli channa (large chickpeas)	240 mL
3 Tbsp.	vegetable oil	45 mL
1 tsp.	ginger paste	5 mL
1 tsp.	garlic paste	5 mL
2	green chilies (chopped)	2
1	onion (finely chopped)	1
1 Tbsp.	cilantro (chopped)	15 mL
1 Tbsp.	khatai (dried mango powder)	15 mL
½ tsp.	salt	2.5 mL
2	large potatoes (boiled and cut into small pieces)	2
2	lemons (squeezed)	2
1	small onion (blended)	1
¼ tsp.	red food coloring	1.2 mL
1 Tbsp.	tamarind pulp (optional)	15 mL
1 tsp.	chaat masala (see page 23)	5 mL

Punjabi Chole is usually served as a side dish with various other curries, chapatis, pakoras or raitas. It is perfect on a quiet relaxing weekend afternoon. Although the recipe says to use fresh large chickpeas, using canned chickpeas will not affect the flavor of this dish in any way. (Use two 19 oz/ 540 mL cans.)

1. Soak the chickpeas overnight in a large pot with at least 6 inches (15 cm) water above the level of the beans.
2. Next day, pressure-cook the chickpeas for at least 20 minutes or boil for 35–50 minutes, until tender.
3. In another pot heat oil on medium high heat and add the ginger paste, garlic paste, green chilies, onion and cilantro and fry for 2 minutes.
4. Add the khatai and salt. Now add the chickpeas and boiled potatoes.
5. Add the freshly squeezed lemon. Cover and simmer for 10–15 minutes.
6. To garnish, blend the small onion with red food coloring and a little tamarind pulp (if using).
7. To decorate, drizzle this mixture over the kabuli chana. Sprinkle with chaat masala.

Serves 4

Chicken and Meat Dishes

East Indian cuisine is a celebration of flavors from many cultures and nationalities. Many Indians from the North and South have a vast repertoire of rich meat dishes. However, the truly heavenly curries made without using thickening agents such as corn starch or onions, originate from the home of the Indian Muslims, mostly from Hyderabaad, Delhi and Lucknow.

These recipes can be prepared using either chicken or lamb. Most of them also require special preparation—for example, they may need to be marinated overnight to lock in the rich flavors, or may require slow simmering with delicious and exotic sauces. For tips on preparing chicken, see page viii.

When meat is marinated with yogurt, ginger and garlic, or salt, the cooking time is always reduced by at least 10–15 minutes.

Whatever your taste preferences, these exotic recipes are sure to make your next party one to remember.

Almond Chicken

2 lbs.	chicken breasts	900 g
6–8	cloves garlic	6–8
2 inch	piece ginger	5 cm
3–4	green chilies	3–4
2	medium onions	2
2 Tbsp.	vegetable oil	30 mL
1 1/2 cups	yogurt	360 mL
1 tsp.	salt	5 mL
2	bay leaves	2
1 tsp.	dhania (coriander powder)	5 mL
1 tsp.	jeera (cumin powder)	5 mL
2 Tbsp.	crispy fried onions (see page 54)	30 mL
1/4 tsp.	mace powder	1.2 mL
1/4 tsp.	cardamom powder	1.2 mL
1/4 tsp.	cinnamon powder	1.2 mL
1/2 cup	whipping cream or half-and-half	120 mL
15	almonds (whole)	15

This dry chicken dish is soo-oo good that it's difficult to know when to stop eating. It tastes even better the next day when served with Raita (see page 95) and roast potatoes.

1. Cut chicken breasts into 8 pieces.
2. Make a paste of the garlic, ginger and green chilies in a food processor.
3. Slice the onions and fry in hot vegetable oil in a saucepan until golden brown. Drain and grind to a paste, reserving frying oil for step 5.
4. Mix the yogurt with salt and the two pastes, and use as marinade for chicken. Allow to marinate for 2 hours.
5. Using the vegetable oil in which the onions were fried, add the bay leaves and fry the chicken on low heat until cooked and brown.
6. Mix together the coriander powder, cumin powder and fried onions in 1/2 cup (120 mL) of water. Add this to the cooked chicken. Cover the pot tightly so that the steam does not escape. Simmer for 15 minutes.
7. Uncover and sprinkle over the mace, cardamom and cinnamon. Add whipping cream (or half-and-half).
8. Transfer from saucepan to serving dish and garnish with almonds.

Serve with Masala Puris (see page 112).

Serves 4–6

Tandoori Chicken (p. 74) with Naan (p. 114) and Raita (p. 95)

Clockwise from top: Nariyal Mohogo (p. 33) and Pasande (p. 67) with Chapati (p. 108)

Sheesh Kebabs with Tomato Gravy (p. 72)

Clockwise from top: Daal Curry (p. 40), Potato Curry (p. 29), Yeast Dahi Paratha (p. 120) and Chicken Palak (p. 63)

Butter Chicken

This rich Moghlai dish is perhaps the most popular East Indian dish among North Americans. Butter Chicken is not only my sister Jenny's favorite dish, it is also very popular in my advanced cooking class. Once you try it, I guarantee it will be your favorite too.

1. Prick the chicken pieces with a fork and rub with the ginger paste, garlic paste, chili powder, turmeric, tandoori powder and salt. Let it sit for half an hour.
2. In a saucepan melt 2 Tbsp. (30 mL) of the ghee or clarified butter to medium high heat. Add the crispy fried onions and chicken and fry until the chicken is golden brown. Add 1 cup (240 mL) of warm water and cook for 15 minutes or until chicken is tender.
3. Meanwhile in a frying pan heat the remaining 4 Tbsp. (60 mL) ghee or clarified butter on medium high heat. Fry the raisins and blanched almonds for 1 minute then put aside.
4. Add the 1 cup (240 mL) thick milk to the chicken and cook uncovered on low until milk is absorbed.
5. Add Worcestershire sauce, sugar, cardamom and nutmeg.
6. Add the whipping cream, raisins and almonds. Bring to a boil and then remove from heat.

Serve with rice or naan.

Serves 6

2 lbs.	whole chicken cut in 2-inch (5-cm) slices	900 g
1 tsp.	ginger paste	5 mL
1 tsp.	garlic paste	5 mL
1/2 tsp.	chili powder	2.5 mL
1/4 tsp.	haldi (turmeric)	1.2 mL
1 Tbsp.	tandoori powder	15 mL
3/4 tsp.	salt	4 mL
6 Tbsp.	ghee or clarified butter	90 mL
4 Tbsp.	crispy fried onions (see page 54)	60 mL
1 cup	water (warm)	240 mL
1/2 cup	raisins	120 mL
1/4 cup	blanched almonds	60 mL
4 1/4 cups	milk boiled to 1 cup (240 mL)	1 L
1 1/2 Tbsp.	Worcestershire sauce	22.5 mL
2 tsp.	sugar	10 mL
1/2 tsp.	cardamom powder	2.5 mL
1/2 tsp.	nutmeg	2.5 mL
3/4 cup	whipping cream	180 mL

Spicy Buttered Chicken

1 lb.	chicken (thighs and legs)	455 g
1 Tbsp.	tandoori masala powder	15 mL
1 cup	yogurt	240 mL
2 tsp.	salt	10 mL
1 tsp.	ground black pepper	5 mL
2	medium tomatoes	2
1	green chili	1
1	onion (chopped)	1
1 tsp.	ginger paste	5 mL
½ tsp.	chili powder	2.5 mL
1 Tbsp.	butter	15 mL
1 cup	whipping cream or sour cream	240 mL
¼ cup	roasted ground cashew nuts	60 mL
¼ cup	cilantro (chopped)	60 mL
2 Tbsp.	crispy fried onions (see page 54)	30 mL

A rich chicken dish cooked with butter, cream and cashew nuts. Half-and-half or yogurt can be used in place of cream and almonds can be used instead of cashews.

1. Marinate the chicken in the tandoori masala, yogurt, salt and black pepper for an hour.
2. Blend tomatoes, green chili, onion, ginger paste and chili powder.
3. In a saucepan, heat butter on medium high and add ground tomato mixture to it. Let it boil until thick.
4. Add the marinated chicken and let it cook slowly until the chicken is tender and almost dry, approximately 20 minutes.
5. Add the cream or sour cream and cashew nuts. Let cook for 2–3 minutes until done.
6. Garnish with coriander leaves and fried onions.

Serve with Yeast Dahi Parathas (see page 120) or Dahi Parathas (see page 119).

Serves 6

Chicken à la King

A wonderful meal of creamy chicken with yogurt and green chilies. This is my own version of this curry with green chilies. It is also a big favorite among my friends in Tanzania.

1. Boil the chicken in 1 cup (240 mL) of water with the garlic and ginger pastes for 25 minutes or until tender. Shred the chicken. Keep stock aside.
2. In a saucepan, heat the margarine on medium high. Add the bell pepper and cook until limp.
3. Add the salt, pepper and flour. Stir for 1 minute. Add the stock and stir continuously until it thickens.
4. Add the yogurt and shredded chicken. Cook for 5 minutes on medium heat.
5. Add the beaten egg into the chicken mixture and cook for 2 more minutes, stirring all the time.
6. Put onto serving plate and garnish with grated carrot, sliced boiled eggs and chopped green chilies.

Serve with Bhagharay Chawal (Plain Fried Rice, see page 122) and Carrot Pickles (see page 96).

Serves 5

2 lbs.	chicken (whole chicken cut into pieces)	900 g
1 cup	water	240 mL
1 tsp.	garlic paste	5 mL
1 tsp.	ginger paste	5 mL
1 Tbsp.	margarine	15 mL
1	green bell pepper (chopped)	1
1 tsp.	salt	5 mL
1 tsp.	black pepper	5 mL
2 Tbsp.	all-purpose flour	30 mL
2 cups	yogurt	475 mL
1	egg (beaten)	1
1	carrot (grated)	1
2	boiled eggs (sliced)	2
1 tsp.	green chilies (chopped)	5 mL

Chicken Curry

2 ½ lbs.	whole chicken	1.1 kg
3 Tbsp.	vegetable oil	45 mL
½ tsp.	ginger paste	2.5 mL
½ tsp.	garlic (crushed)	2.5 mL
1	medium tomato (chopped)	1
1 tsp.	curry powder	5 mL
1 Tbsp.	salt	15 mL
4 Tbsp.	yogurt (optional)	60 mL
4	medium potatoes (cut up) (optional)	4
4 Tbsp.	crispy fried onions (see below)	60 mL
¼ tsp.	chili powder (optional)	1.2 mL
½ tsp.	garam masala	2.5 mL
2 Tbsp.	cilantro (chopped)	30 mL
½ tsp.	saffron	2.5 mL

 Crispy fried onions are sold in packages in East Indian grocery stores. They can also be prepared by slicing onions into thin circles, heating oil in a pan and deep-frying them until they turn golden brown. Remove them from the pan, drain and cool on a baking tray. Store in an airtight container for up to 8 months.

*E*very East Indian home has its own version of chicken curry. Try our version using ingredients specially combined to bring out the richness of this fairly simple chicken dish. The richness is enough to make anyone believe a gourmet chef prepared it, but the simplicity allows even a novice to cook it. Saffron, which is a key ingredient in this recipe, is perhaps the most expensive spice in the world.

1. Cut chicken into small curry size pieces.
2. In a large saucepan, heat oil on medium high. Add the ginger paste, garlic, tomato and curry powder. Fry for 1 minute.
3. Add the chicken pieces, salt and yogurt (if using) and cook for 20 minutes.
4. Add the potatoes and cook until potatoes and meat are tender—approximately 25 minutes.
5. Add the crispy fried onions, chili powder (if using), garam masala, chopped cilantro and saffron. Let simmer for 5 minutes before serving.

Serve hot.

Serves 4

Chicken Delight

This is a special favorite, brought to you from my kitchen. Chicken Delight makes a wonderful brunch dish and is best enjoyed straight from the oven.

1. Boil chicken in the 1 cup (240 mL) of water with the garam masala for 25 minutes (uncovered).
2. Heat butter in a separate saucepan. Add flour and stir until golden brown.
3. Remove from heat. Gradually add milk, stirring all the time.
4. Add salt, pepper, chopped parsley and chopped green chilies or chili powder.
5. Return to heat and continue cooking on low until fairly thick.
6. Remove from the heat and add the beaten egg yolk. Stir thoroughly.
7. Add lemon juice and let the sauce cool.
8. Heat oven to 400°F (200°C).
9. Dip chicken pieces in the sauce and let them cool completely.
10. Place the chicken in a greased ovenproof dish.
11. Coat each piece of chicken with the cheese. Bake for 20 minutes or until brown on both sides.

Serve hot.

Serves 4

2 lbs.	whole chicken cut into 8 pieces	900 g
1 cup	water	240 mL
1/2 tsp.	garam masala	2.5 mL
1 Tbsp.	butter	15 mL
1 Tbsp.	all-purpose flour	15 mL
1 3/4 cups	milk	420 mL
1/4 tsp.	salt	1.2 mL
1/4 tsp.	black pepper	1.2 mL
1 Tbsp.	parsley (finely chopped)	15 mL
2	green chilies (or 1/2 tsp./2.5 mL chili powder)	2
1	egg yolk (beaten)	1
1 tsp.	fresh lemon juice	5 mL
1 1/2 cups	grated cheese	360 mL

Chicken Khandari Kofta

½ tsp.	cinnamon powder	2.5 mL
1 tsp.	salt	5 mL
1 lb.	chicken (ground)	455 g
3 Tbsp.	vegetable oil	45 mL
2	large onions (boiled)	2
1 tsp.	ginger paste	5 mL
1 tsp.	garlic paste	5 mL
1 Tbsp.	dhania (coriander powder)	15 mL
1 tsp.	red chili powder	5 mL
½ cup	tomato paste	120 mL
¾ cup	cashew nut paste (see below)	180 mL
1 ½ cups	water	360 mL
½ tsp.	garam masala	2.5 mL
2 Tbsp.	pomegranate syrup	30 mL
½ cup	whipping cream or half-and-half	120 mL

Pomegranate syrup is a specialty item and can be found in most Middle Eastern grocery stores.

Cashew nut paste can be prepared by soaking ½ cup (120 mL) of cashew nuts in water for half an hour and later grinding to a smooth paste in a food processor.

*T*his dish is a unique combination of curry powder and pomegranate syrup—an unlikely pairing but delicious all the same and a favorite of my daughter Fatima. This curry has a rich creamy texture due to the cashew nut paste and cream.

1. Mix together the cinnamon powder, salt and ground chicken.
2. Divide the chicken mixture into 12 golf ball-sized meatballs and set aside.
3. In a saucepan heat the oil to medium high. Blend the boiled onions in a food processor to form a paste and cook until it turns light brown.
4. Add the ginger and garlic pastes and sauté for 1 minute.
5. Add coriander powder, red chili powder, tomato paste and the cashew nut paste and cook on high heat, stirring constantly, for at least 2 minutes. Add water and bring to boil.
6. Add the meatballs and cook for 10 minutes, stirring occasionally. (Do not break the meatballs.)
7. Add the garam masala and pomegranate syrup.
8. Simmer for 5 minutes and stir in cream.

Serve with either rice and green vegetables, or naan or parathas.

Serves 4

Chicken with Peanut Butter

*T*he flavor of the peanut butter infuses into the chicken when it is simmering. This is a real specialty dish.

1. Cut the chicken into small pieces.
2. Heat the vegetable oil in a saucepan on medium high and fry chicken until golden brown.
3. Add the onions, chilies, salt and tomatoes. Cook until onions become transparent and limp.
4. Now add peanut butter and mix well.
5. Add water to form a sauce. Simmer until chicken is done (about 20 minutes).

Serve on a bed of rice.

Serves 6

2 lbs.	whole chicken	900 g
4 Tbsp.	vegetable oil	60 mL
4	onions (chopped)	4
5	green chilies (chopped)	5
½ tsp.	salt	2.5 mL
3	tomatoes (chopped)	3
5 Tbsp.	smooth peanut butter	75 mL
1 cup	water	240 mL

Chicken Xacuti

2 lbs.	whole chicken	900 g
½ cup	vegetable oil	120 mL
1 cup	grated coconut	240 mL
2	cinnamon sticks (1 inch/2.5 cm)	2
6	cloves	6
4	dried red chilies	4
½ tsp.	haldi (turmeric seeds)	2.5 mL
2 Tbsp.	khus khus (poppy seeds)	30 mL
1 tsp.	ajwain (carom seeds)	5 mL
1 tsp.	jeera (cumin seeds)	5 mL
1 tsp.	peppercorns	5 mL
1 tsp.	fennel seeds	5 mL
4	star anise	4
1 Tbsp.	dhania (coriander seeds)	15 mL
4	cloves garlic	4
2	medium onions	2
2 cups	water	475 mL
1 tsp.	salt	5 mL
1 Tbsp.	tamarind pulp	15 mL
¼ tsp.	grated nutmeg	1.2 mL

Tandoori Naan can be purchased at any East Indian grocery store.

A combination of three sets of masalas—whole spice, dry roasted and tempered—all ground into a fine paste go into this specialty chicken in a very rich gravy. By the way, it's pronounced "shakuty."

1. Remove the skin from the chicken and cut into 12 pieces. Set aside.
2. In a saucepan, heat ¼ cup (60 mL) of the oil to medium high. Fry the coconut until almost brown.
3. On a thick griddle on medium heat, dry roast the cinnamon, cloves, red chilies, turmeric, poppy seeds, carom seeds, cumin seeds, peppercorns, fennel seeds, star anise and coriander seeds.
4. Grind the roasted ingredients with the garlic and coconut.
5. Peel and chop the onions. Heat the remaining ¼ cup (60 mL) oil on medium high and fry the onions until light brown. Add the ground spices and cook until the oil separates. Then add the chicken pieces and fry for 2–3 minutes.
6. Add the water and salt and bring to boil for about 10 minutes and then add tamarind and nutmeg.
7. Simmer for 5 minutes more.

Serve with rice or tandoori naan and green salad.

Serves 6

Coconut Milk Fried Chicken

*T*his classic curry is a favorite of almost all my students. Try serving it with parathas (see pages 117–120) and Onion Salad (see page 103) and prepare for an enthusiastic response.

1. Prepare the masala powder by roasting the ingredients on a dry frying pan over medium heat. Cool, then grind in a coffee grinder.
2. Clean the chicken and remove the skin. Cut into 16 pieces and add 1 tsp. (5 mL) salt. Set aside.
3. Grind the chilies, garlic, ginger and vinegar into a masala paste. Mix the masala paste with the coconut milk.
4. Combine the chicken mixture and the masala paste in a large saucepan. Add the masala powder, chili powder and lemon juice to the chicken. Cook on low heat for 20 minutes.
5. Once cooked, remove the chicken pieces from the gravy. Keep the gravy aside.
6. Peel and slice the potatoes into long thin strips. Fry in the ½ cup (120 mL) oil and remove.
7. Fry the cooked chicken pieces in the same oil until golden brown. Remove and keep aside.
8. Dice and then fry onion in the same oil until golden brown. Add curry leaves and chili powder to the fried onions. Pour in the gravy and stir until it thickens. Add salt to taste.
9. Place the fried chicken pieces in a serving dish and pour gravy over it.

Serve hot with fried potatoes.

Serves 4–6

Ingredients for masala powder:

2–3	red chilies	2–3
½ inch	piece ginger	1.2 cm
2	cinnamon sticks (2 inches/10 cm)	2
3	cardamom pods	3
6	cloves	6
1 tsp.	aniseed	5 mL

Main ingredients:

2 lbs.	whole chicken	900 g
1 tsp.	salt	5 mL
2–3	green chilies	2–3
2–3	cloves garlic	2–3
½ inch	piece ginger	1.2 cm
2 Tbsp.	white vinegar	30 mL
2 cups	coconut milk	475 mL
½ tsp.	chili powder	2.5 mL
2 Tbsp.	fresh lemon juice	30 mL
3	medium potatoes	3
½ cup	vegetable oil	120 mL
3	medium onions	3
6	limro (fresh curry leaves)	6
¼ tsp.	chili powder	1.2 mL

Cream Chicken

1 tsp.	salt	5 mL
2 lbs.	chicken (cut into curry pieces)	900 g
3 Tbsp.	vegetable oil	45 mL
1 tsp.	garlic paste	5 mL
1 tsp.	ginger paste	5 mL
1	green chili (chopped)	1
1 tsp.	whole jeera (black cumin seeds)	5 mL
2 cups	yogurt or half-and-half cream	475 mL
3	cardamom pods (ground)	3
8	black peppercorns	8

This curry has been a longtime favorite at my mom's place from the time we were young. Now it is enjoyed by three generations of the family. Thanks, Mom.

1. Salt the chicken pieces and leave for half an hour.
2. Heat oil to medium high in a pan. Add the garlic paste, ginger paste, chopped chili and cumin.
3. Add the chicken pieces and stir-fry for 2–3 minutes then cook on low heat for approximately 15 minutes. You may have to add a little water to cook the chicken longer if not done.
4. Add the yogurt or cream and stir gently for 30 seconds.
5. Lastly add the ground cardamom and black pepper to give it that special aroma.

Serve with rice or rotis.

Serves 4

Simply Indian

Do Piyaza (Spiced Lamb or Mutton with Onions)

This dish can be prepared a day ahead to let the spices mature. It can also be frozen for 3–4 months. When ready to serve again, you can microwave it. In India, young goat's meat is considered lamb and adult goat's meat is called mutton.

1. Heat the ghee or vegetable oil in a heavy pan over medium high heat. Add the onions and fry gently until soft (about 2 minutes).
2. Remove half of the onions from the pan, add the spices, and fry for a few more minutes.
3. Add the chilies and meat and fry until meat is brown. Add approximately 2 cups (475 mL) of water and cook partially covered for 1 hour or until meat is tender.
4. Add the reserved onion and garam masala and simmer for 5 minutes or until curry is fairly thick.

Serve hot with rice and a pickle and salad of your choice.

Serves 4–6

2 Tbsp.	ghee or vegetable oil	30 mL
3	large onions (sliced)	3
2 tsp.	ground jeera (cumin seeds)	10 mL
1 tsp.	ground methi (fenugreek)	5 mL
1 tsp.	haldi (turmeric powder)	5 mL
3	green chilies (chopped)	3
2 1/2 lbs.	lamb or mutton (any part), cut into cubes	1.1 kg
2 cups	water	475 mL
1 tsp.	garam masala	5 mL

Hara Ghost

This is a very famous Rajasthani dish.

2 lbs.	spinach	900 g
1 cup	fresh mint leaves or ½ cup (120 mL) dried, soaked in water	240 mL
2 Tbsp.	vegetable oil	30 mL
2	onions (chopped)	2
2 lbs.	boneless beef (cut into stew pieces)	900 g
1 cup	yogurt	240 mL
1 tsp.	salt	5 mL

Grind the following to a paste using a food processor:

1 tsp.	garlic paste	5 mL
1 tsp.	ginger paste	5 mL
1 tsp.	jeera (cumin seeds)	5 mL
1 tsp.	dhania (coriander seeds)	5 mL
3	green chilies (chopped)	3

1. Wash and clean the spinach and fresh mint leaves thoroughly. If using dried mint, soak in water for 10–15 minutes, long enough to soak the leaves. Extract the juice by grinding in a food processor. Set the juice aside.
2. Heat the vegetable oil on medium high heat. Fry the onions until golden brown.
3. Add the meat along with the ground paste. Stir and fry for a few minutes.
4. Stir in the yogurt and salt. Cover and cook over low heat, stirring from time to time.
5. After 30 minutes, pour in the spinach and mint juice. Mix thoroughly then cover with a lid and cook until meat is tender (approximately 20 minutes).

Serve hot, garnished with onion rings.

Serves 6

Mutton, Chicken or Beef Palak

*T*his dish can be prepared using mutton, chicken or beef. *Keep in mind that, although boneless meat seems easier to handle, meat on the bone will enhance the flavor. If the bunches of spinach are small, use two because the rich creamy texture of this dish is due to the spinach used in the sauce.*

Method for roasted masala:

1. In a small pan, dry roast all masala ingredients.
2. Let cool 5 minutes.
3. Grind in a coffee grinder.

Method for palak:

1. Boil the meat in a large saucepan with half the garlic and ginger pastes and all the water. Let it cook until tender (approximately 25 minutes) and only 1 ½ cups (360 mL) of stock remains. Set aside.
2. While the meat is cooking, boil the chopped spinach, cool and grind in a food processor. Set aside for step 6.
3. Heat the oil on medium high in a large pan. Fry the onions until golden.
4. Add the remaining garlic paste and ginger paste, chopped tomatoes and roasted masala. Reduce heat to low. Cook until the oil rises to the surface.
5. Add the meat and the remaining stock. Cook for 5 minutes.
6. Add the spinach to the meat and simmer for 5 minutes.
7. Stir in the lemon juice.

Serve with rice or naan.

Serves 8

Ingredients for roasted masala:

1 tsp.	jeera (cumin seeds)	5 mL
1 tsp.	dhania (coriander seeds)	5 mL
1 Tbsp.	desiccated coconut	15 mL
2	red chilies (dried)	2

Ingredients for palak:

2 lbs.	chicken or mutton, cut into curry pieces	900 g
1 tsp.	garlic paste	5 mL
1 tsp.	ginger paste	5 mL
4 cups	water	950 mL
2 Tbsp.	vegetable oil	30 mL
2	medium onions (chopped)	2
2	medium tomatoes (chopped)	2
1 Tbsp.	roasted masala	15 mL
1	bunch of spinach (finely chopped)	1
1 Tbsp.	fresh lemon juice	15 mL

Kashmiri Chicken

2 lbs.	whole chicken	900 g
2 Tbsp.	fried onions	30 mL
2–3	green chilies	2–3
3	tomatoes	3
1 tsp.	garlic paste	5 mL
1 tsp.	ginger paste	5 mL
3 Tbsp.	fresh lemon juice	45 mL
1 1/2 tsp.	curry powder	7.5 mL
1 tsp.	red chili powder	5 mL
2 Tbsp.	garam masala	30 mL
2 Tbsp.	coconut (desiccated and unsweetened)	30 mL
1 tsp.	salt	5 mL
1/2 tsp.	haldi (turmeric)	2.5 mL
1/4 cup	vegetable oil	60 mL
2 cups	yogurt	475 mL
1/4 cup	chopped parsley (for sprinkling)	60 mL

This mild unique Kashmiri dish is my own personal recipe. It is one of the few dry dishes that make use of yogurt.

1. Heat oven to 375°F (190°C).
2. Wash and cut chicken into 8 pieces and put into a baking pan.
3. Blend the fried onions, green chilies, tomatoes, garlic paste, ginger paste, freshly squeezed lemon juice, curry powder, red chili powder, garam masala, coconut, salt and turmeric in a food processor, then add the vegetable oil and yogurt.
4. Pour the mixture over the chicken pieces.
5. Bake for approximately 40 minutes.

Serve with fried potatoes on a bed of yellow rice sprinkled with parsley.

Serves 4

Mutton or Chicken Corn Bake

This mouth-watering dish was adapted from an old recipe of my mom's, and is a "potluck" family favorite. It is also a long-time favorite dish of my husband, Mohammed.

1. Heat oven to 350°F (175°C).
2. Heat 1 Tbsp. (15 mL) of the butter or margarine and sauté the bell pepper and green chilies. Add the meat and corn and cook for about 3 minutes.
3. To make the white sauce, heat the remaining 1 Tbsp. (15 mL) of butter or margarine in a saucepan and add ½ cup (120 mL) of all-purpose flour. Fry for about 1 minute (be careful not to let it brown), then add the 2 cups (475 mL) of milk and the stock, stirring continuously. Add a pinch of salt and ground pepper for seasoning and cook for at least 5 minutes to make sure the starch has cooked properly and the sauce has thickened.
4. Add to the meat mixture.
5. Add half the cheese, keeping the remainder aside for topping.
6. Boil over low heat until thick.
7. Pour the mixture into a slightly greased ovenproof dish.
8. Sprinkle grated cheese over top.
9. Bake for 15–20 minutes.

Serves 6

2 Tbsp.	butter or margarine	30 mL
½ cup	bell pepper, any color or assorted (chopped)	120 mL
2	green chilies (chopped)	2
1 cup	mutton or chicken (boiled and shredded or cubed)	1
1 cup	frozen corn	240 mL
½ cup	all-purpose flour	120 mL
2 cups	milk	475 mL
1 cup	stock (see below)	240 mL
	pinch of salt (for seasoning)	
	pinch of pepper (for seasoning)	
1 cup	grated cheese (cheddar or mozzarella)	240 mL

 If you are making Chicken Corn Bake, use chicken stock, and if you are making Mutton Corn Bake, use mutton stock.

Oyster Chicken

This chicken dish is another family favorite and my son-in-law Sibtain's favorite.

2 lbs.	whole chicken	900 g
1 Tbsp.	soy sauce	15 mL
½ tsp.	black pepper	2.5 mL
½ tsp.	salt	2.5 mL
1 Tbsp.	corn oil	15 mL
½ tsp.	ginger paste	2.5 mL
½ tsp.	garlic paste	2.5 mL
2 Tbsp.	corn flour	30 mL
¼ cup	water	60 mL
1 inch	piece ginger (julienned)	2.5 cm
1 Tbsp.	oyster sauce	15 mL
½ cup	green onions (chopped)	120 mL

1. Cut the chicken into 8 pieces. Marinate in the soy sauce, black pepper and salt for one hour.
2. In a large pot heat the oil to medium high heat and add the ginger, garlic and chicken. Fry over low heat until chicken is cooked (approximately 20 minutes), stirring all the time.
3. In a bowl, mix the corn flour with ¼ cup (60 mL) water and pour over the cooked chicken. Simmer for 5 minutes.
4. Add the ginger, oyster sauce and green onions.
5. If the mix is dry you may add ½ cup (120 mL) of water and 1 Tbsp. (15 mL) soy sauce.

Serve with rice.

Serves 6

Pasande

A specialty of the Nawabs in India, this is also my specialty for family and guests on special occasions. Due to the richness of the dish, it is best served with either plain rice or chapatis.

1. Cut the meat into thin slices and beat them until they are thin and flat.
2. Marinate them in the yogurt, ginger paste, garlic paste and salt for 1 hour.
3. Heat the oil in a large saucepan to medium hot and fry the onions until golden brown. Remove from the oil and, when cool, crush to a powder.
4. In a blender or food processor grind the poppy seeds, almonds, saffron, coriander seeds, chilies and turmeric to a fine paste, adding ½ cup (120 mL) of the water.
5. In the same saucepan that you fried the onions, put the meat and the blended spices. Cover and cook on low heat until the meat is tender and the gravy is dry.
6. Add the powdered fried onions, garam masala, remaining ½ cup (120 mL) of water and the kewra essence. Do not make it watery, this is supposed to be a dry dish.

Sprinkle with chopped cilantro and garnish with egg slices before serving.

Serves 3–4

2 lbs.	beef tenderloin	900 g
2 cups	yogurt	475 mL
1 ½ tsp.	ginger paste	7.5 mL
1 ½ tsp.	garlic paste	7.5 mL
½ tsp.	salt	2.5 mL
4 Tbsp.	vegetable oil	60 mL
3	large onions (sliced)	3
2 Tbsp.	khus khus (poppy seeds)	30 mL
26	almonds (peeled)	26
½ tsp.	saffron	2.5 mL
1 tsp.	dhania (coriander seeds)	5 mL
3	green chilies	3
½ tsp.	haldi (turmeric)	2.5 mL
1 cup	water	240 mL
1 ½ tsp.	garam masala	7.5 mL
1 tsp.	kewra essence	5 mL
¼ cup	cilantro (chopped)	60 mL
2	hard-boiled eggs (sliced)	2

 Kewra essence is found in almost all East Indian grocery stores.

Peppery Chicken

A semi-dry chicken masala cooked with tomatoes and tamarind sauce with a spicy flavor of peppercorns.

2 lbs.	chicken	900 g
2	medium onions	2
3	medium tomatoes	3
3 tsp.	crushed peppercorns	15 mL
2	red chilies	2
1 tsp.	ginger paste	5 mL
1 tsp.	garlic paste	5 mL
1 tsp.	red chili powder	5 mL
1 Tbsp.	fresh lemon juice	15 mL
1 tsp.	haldi (turmeric)	5 mL
1 tsp.	salt	5 mL
5 Tbsp.	vegetable oil	75 mL
12	limro (fresh curry leaves)	12
2 tsp.	dhania powder (coriander powder)	10 mL
1 Tbsp.	tamarind pulp (see below)	15 mL
1 tsp.	garam masala	5 mL
2 Tbsp.	cilantro (chopped)	30 mL

1. Wash and skin the chicken and cut into pieces. (Boneless chicken can also be used.)
2. Peel and chop the onions and tomatoes. Set aside.
3. Make a paste of the peppercorns, red chilies, ginger, garlic and chili powder by mixing them together.
4. Marinate the chicken in the paste for 3 hours. Mix in the lemon juice, turmeric and salt.
5. Heat the oil to high and fry the marinated chicken until brown. Set aside.
6. Fry the onions in the same oil until light brown. Add the curry leaves and stir.
7. Add the tomatoes and coriander powder and fry until the oil rises to the surface of the masala.
8. Add the chicken and a little water. Cover and cook until chicken is coated with masala.
9. Add tamarind pulp dissolved in ½ cup (120 mL) of water.
10. Simmer for 10 minutes, stirring occasionally. Add garam masala and chopped cilantro.

Serve with naan or rice.

Serves 4

Tamarind is found in most Chinese and Indian grocery stores. It comes in packages already in pulp form. Tamarind sauce (aamli sauce) can also be prepared as follows:

1. Soak ½ cup (120 mL) of tamarind pulp in 1 cup (240 mL) of boiling water. Extract juice by straining out all pulp through a sieve. Add ¼ tsp. (1.2 mL) salt and ¼ tsp. (1.2 mL) red chili powder and mix well.

2. Pour the sauce in a glass jar. This can be refrigerated for one week.

Safed Masalam Murg (Dry Chicken Curry)

This is a dry delicate dish. It derives its flavor from the yogurt and spices. It is rather an unusual combination of flavors, but I recommend you try it for a wonderful weekend luncheon or family get-together.

1. Mix the yogurt, 1 tsp. (5 mL) of the garam masala, chili powder, garlic paste, ginger paste and salt. Use to marinate the chicken and set aside for half an hour.
2. Soak the onion rings in vinegar in a separate bowl.
3. Heat the vegetable oil to medium high. Sauté the remaining onions. Add the cinnamon stick, cloves, cumin and ground pepper. (This is Whole Garam Masala.) Cook this for 2 minutes until a pleasant aroma is released.
4. Add the marinated chicken and cook until half done, about 10 minutes for pieces or 20 minutes for whole chicken. Then add the onion rings with the vinegar.
5. Chicken is cooked when the liquid has evaporated and the meat is tender.

Serves 6

2 cups	yogurt	475 mL
2 tsp.	garam masala	10 mL
1 tsp.	chili powder	5 mL
1 tsp.	garlic paste	5 mL
1 tsp.	ginger paste	5 mL
1 tsp.	salt	5 mL
2 lbs.	chicken (whole or cut in pieces)	900 g
2	medium onions (sliced into rings)	2
3 Tbsp.	white vinegar	45 mL
3 Tbsp.	vegetable oil	45 mL
2	onions (cut lengthwise)	2
1	cinnamon stick (approximately 2 inches/5 cm)	1
3	whole cloves	3
1 tsp.	jeera (cumin) (coarsely ground)	5 mL
1 tsp.	ground black pepper	5 mL

Kebabs à la Balkan

Ingredients for kebabs:

2 lbs.	fillet meat (cubed—your choice of meat)	900 g
½ tsp.	salt	2.5 mL
4 cups	water	950 mL
1 tsp.	garlic paste	5 mL
1 lb.	carrots (cut into rounds)	455 g
2	medium onions (cubed)	2
1	green bell pepper (cubed)	1
1 dozen	skewers (bamboo if available, or metal)	1 dozen

Ingredients for sauce:

3 Tbsp.	vegetable oil	45 mL
3	tomatoes (crushed)	3
1 Tbsp.	jeera (cumin)	15 mL
1 Tbsp.	fresh lemon juice	15 mL
1 tsp.	ginger (crushed)	5 mL
1 tsp.	garlic (crushed)	5 mL
1 tsp.	haldi (turmeric)	5 mL
2 cups	stock from boiled meat	475 mL

Meat or chicken kebab skewers with spicy gravy make a delicious meal on a bed of sweet and sour rice. This is my daughter Fatima's favorite dish.

Method for kebabs:
1. Boil meat in salt, water and garlic paste until tender, approximately 15 minutes.
2. Add the carrots and cook for 5 minutes more. Reserve 2 cups (475 mL) of stock.
3. Skewer in the following order: meat, bell pepper, meat, onion, carrot and meat.

Method for sauce:
1. In a large saucepan, heat oil on medium high. Mix in all the sauce ingredients except the stock.
2. Cook for a few minutes until thick.
3. Add meat stock and slowly place all the skewers in the sauce.
4. Cook over very low heat and let the onions and bell pepper become soft. Turn them to the other side. Cook for 2 minutes and remove. Repeat until all the skewers are cooked.
5. Remove the sauce from heat, return all the skewers to it and set aside while preparing the rice.

Method for rice:

1. Boil rice in salt water and set aside.
2. Heat butter or oil and add the green onions and bell pepper.
3. Cook until the onions are soft.
4. In a bowl mix together the vinegar, ketchup and pepper.
5. Add to the boiled rice and mix until it is pink in color.
6. Mix all these in the pan with the onions and bell pepper. Mix lightly so that the rice grains do not break.

Serve the skewers on a bed of salad and rice. Pour sauce on top of the skewers.

Serves 5

Ingredients for rice:

2 cups	basmati rice	475 mL
6 cups	water	1.5 L
1 tsp.	salt	5 mL
2 Tbsp.	vegetable oil, butter or margarine	30 mL
1	bunch of green onions (chopped)	1
½ cup	green bell pepper (finely chopped)	120 mL
3 Tbsp.	white vinegar	45 mL
1 cup	tomato ketchup	240 mL
1 tsp.	black pepper	5 mL

Chicken and Meat Dishes

Sheesh Kebabs with Tomato Gravy

Ingredients for kebabs:

1 lb.	minced meat (your preference)	455 g
¼ cup	mint (chopped)	60 mL
2 Tbsp.	yogurt	30 mL
1	egg (beaten)	1
1 tsp.	garlic paste	5 mL
1 tsp.	ginger paste	5 mL
½ cup	breadcrumbs	120 mL
1 tsp.	jeera (cumin seeds)	5 mL
1 Tbsp.	vinegar	15 mL
1 tsp.	salt	5 mL
1 tsp.	black pepper	5 mL
1 tsp.	vegetable oil	5 mL

Ingredients for gravy:

1 cup	crushed tomatoes	240 mL
2 Tbsp.	tomato paste	30 mL
1 Tbsp.	fresh mint	15 mL
1 tsp.	chili powder	5 mL
2 Tbsp.	vinegar	30 mL
1 tsp.	crushed jeera (cumin seeds)	5 mL
2 Tbsp.	vegetable oil	30 mL

Method for kebabs:

1. Mix together the kebab ingredients and marinate for half an hour.
2. Divide the meat mixture into 16–18 sausage-shaped kebabs and lay them on a greased oven tray.
3. Grill on high heat until firm. Turn over and grill the other side.

Method for gravy:

1. Blend together all the gravy ingredients except the cumin and vegetable oil.
2. In a pan, heat the oil to medium high, add the cumin and then the blended ingredients. Let simmer until oil surfaces to the top and the gravy becomes thick.
3. Lay kebabs in serving dish. Pour the gravy over top.
4. Smoke the kebabs by placing hot charcoal on foil in the center of the dish. Pour 1 tsp. (5 mL) oil on charcoal and cover it for few minutes. Then remove and discard the charcoal.
5. Garnish with mint leaves.

Serve with bread or chapatis.

Serves 6

Sweet and Sour Baked Chicken

This was introduced to India by Chinese immigrants. It is truly a delicious, hot and spicy Indo-Chinese dish.

1. Cut chicken into 2-inch (5-cm) pieces. Marinate in the ginger paste and garlic paste for 1–2 hours.
2. Cut green peppers in julienne, chop the onions lengthwise and chop the green chilies.
3. Drain the canned pineapple.
4. Grind the tomatoes very finely in blender.
5. Combine all ingredients in a bowl with the chicken. Leave for 2 hours.
6. Transfer to baking dish and bake in preheated oven at 400°F (200°C) for an hour, until golden brown.

Serve with plain rice or stir-fry vegetables.

Serves 4

2 lbs.	chicken (whole)	900 g
1 tsp.	ginger paste	5 mL
1 tsp.	garlic paste	5 mL
2	large green peppers	2
2	onions or 5 green onions	2
5	green chilies (chopped) (less if you prefer a milder taste)	5
2 cups	(1 can) pineapple chunks	475 mL
4	tomatoes	4
2 Tbsp.	vegetable oil	30 mL
1 Tbsp.	soy sauce	15 mL
1 tsp.	red chili powder	5 mL
1 tsp.	salt	5 mL
1 Tbsp.	white vinegar	15 mL
2 Tbsp.	tomato ketchup	30 mL

Tandoori Chicken
(Indian-Style Barbecued Chicken)

2 ½ lbs.	whole chicken	1.2 kg
½ tsp.	ginger (crushed)	2.5 mL
½ tsp.	garlic (crushed)	2.5 mL
½ tsp.	chili powder (optional)	2.5 mL
1 cup	plain yogurt	240 mL
1 Tbsp.	tomato paste	15 mL
1 Tbsp.	vegetable oil	15 mL
1 tsp.	tandoori powder	5 mL
1 tsp.	salt (or to taste)	5 mL

Tandoori Chicken is one of the most famous Indian dishes. It originated from the Punjab and has been adopted all over the world. Its rich taste and simple preparation make it a very easy dish to make but it must be prepared the evening before you plan to serve it.

1. Cut chicken into 8–10 pieces, wash and pat dry on a tea towel.
2. In a big bowl, mix all the other ingredients together well.
3. Spread evenly all over the chicken pieces and leave to marinate overnight.
4. The next day, 1 hour before serving, grill either under a hot grill or over charcoal.

Serve with pita bread and Raita (see page 95) or Tamarind Chutney served as a sauce (see page 94).

Serves 4

Walnut Chicken

The tantalizing scent of green pepper and garlic will have your mouth watering when you lift the lid on this Indo-Chinese classic. Egg noodles and cucumber slices make an ideal accompaniment.

1. Cut the chicken into 5 pieces and marinate in the soy sauce, salt, vinegar and ginger for about half an hour.
2. Heat the vegetable oil to medium high in a large frying pan. Add the garlic, chopped onion, green pepper and chilies.
3. Add the chicken and stir over high heat for 10 minutes, until done. Then add walnuts and cook for another 5 minutes.
4. When the chicken is cooked, garnish with sliced onions and bell pepper.

Serve with rice or egg noodles.

Serves 4

1 lb.	boneless chicken (breast or thigh)	455 g
1 Tbsp.	soy sauce	15 mL
½ tsp.	salt	2.5 mL
1 Tbsp.	white vinegar	15 mL
1 ½ tsp.	ginger (chopped)	7.5 mL
3 Tbsp.	vegetable oil	45 mL
½ Tbsp.	garlic (chopped)	7.5 mL
1 Tbsp.	onion (chopped)	15 mL
1 Tbsp.	green pepper (chopped)	15 mL
1 tsp.	green chilies (chopped)	5 mL
1 cup	walnuts (crushed)	120 mL
1	small onion (sliced)	1
1	small green bell pepper (sliced)	1

Spicy Meat Gravy

1 tsp.	chili powder	5 mL
1 tsp.	dhania (coriander powder)	5 mL
½ tsp.	jeera (cumin seeds)	2.5 mL
½ tsp.	black pepper	2.5 mL
2	cinnamon sticks (2 inches/5 cm) long	2
3	cloves	3
4	cardamom pods	4
½ tsp.	haldi (turmeric)	2.5 mL
2 lbs.	mutton	900 g
5	medium onions (chopped)	5
1 tsp.	garlic paste	5 mL
1 tsp.	ginger paste	5 mL
¼ cup	white vinegar	60 mL
1 tsp.	salt	5 mL
1 cup	water	240 mL
¼ cup	vegetable oil	60 mL
1 tsp.	rai (black mustard seeds)	5 mL
2	medium onions (chopped)	2
4	limro (fresh curry leaves)	4

1. Make masala by grinding together the chili powder, coriander powder, cumin seeds, pepper, cinnamon, cloves, cardamom and turmeric.
2. Cook the meat in the ground masala, 5 chopped onions, garlic paste, ginger paste, vinegar, salt and 1 cup (240 mL) of water until the meat is tender, approximately 30–35 minutes.
3. In a saucepan, heat the oil on medium high, fry the mustard seeds, and add the 2 remaining chopped onions and some curry leaves. Add the meat and cook for 5 minutes, adding more water if necessary.

Serve with rice or chapatis.

Serves 6

Fish and Seafood

In East Indian cuisine, fish is never plain poached, steamed or boiled. It is either baked or fried with spice. There are fish curries of many kinds—the rich red curries of Bengal, gently spiced kormas with yogurt from Punjab, or Kerala-style with lots of hot chilies (always deseeded) and cooked in coconut milk and local fruits. Note that most recipes require chilies complete with seeds, but I leave it up to you. If you find it too spicy for your palate, you can deseed them.

Tandoori cooking, which was traditionally only for meat, chicken and bread is now being used for fish. A tandoor is a clay oven designed for fast cooking or baking, and able to withstand very high temperatures. When I was traveling around the coastal area of Kerala, I was served a whole fish marinated with spices and cooked in the tandoor, which left me eager to come home and try the recipe myself. It was really delicious, even if the tandoor had to be replaced with a barbecue or grill.

Perhaps I can tempt you with some of my favorite quick and easy seafood recipes.

Fish Biriyani

3 cups	basmati rice	720 mL
2 lbs.	fish (fillet of sole or halibut)	900 g
1 cup	yogurt	240 mL
1 tsp.	garam masala	5 mL
1 tsp.	salt	5 mL
1 tsp.	red chili powder	5 mL
2 Tbsp.	fresh lemon juice	30 mL
1 tsp.	jeera (cumin powder)	5 mL
½ cup	vegetable oil	120 mL
2	onions (chopped)	2
1 tsp.	garlic paste	5 mL
1 tsp.	ginger paste	5 mL
½ tsp.	haldi (turmeric)	2.5 mL
3	tomatoes (crushed)	3
2	green fresh chilies (chopped)	2
12 cups	water	3 L
1 ½ tsp.	salt	7.5 mL
2 Tbsp.	fried onions (for garnishing)	30 mL
¼ tsp.	saffron (soaked in 2 Tbsp./30 mL water)	1.2 mL
2	sprigs of cilantro (chopped)	2

*E*very time I prepare this dish, the aroma of the fish and its spices reminds me of my birthplace in Tanzania. Many varieties of fish found in the Indian Ocean are not available elsewhere, but there are substitutes for all of them. This dish is equally delicious when made with fillets of sole or halibut.

1. Sort, wash and soak rice in water.
2. Cut fish into medium bite-sized pieces. Marinate in the yogurt, garam masala, salt, ½ tsp. (2.5 mL) of the chili powder, lemon juice and cumin for 15 minutes.
3. Heat the oil and fry the onions on medium low heat until golden brown. Add the garlic paste, ginger paste, remaining ½ tsp. (2.5 mL) chili powder and turmeric. Cook for a few seconds. Add the tomatoes and green chilies and cook until the oil appears on top.
4. Add fish with its marinade and stir very gently, making sure the fish pieces are not crushed. Cook for 5 more minutes on low heat and set aside.
5. Boil rice in 12 cups (3 L) of salted water until tender, approximately 12 minutes. Drain.
6. In a large, heavy, ovenproof saucepan with a lid, pour in ⅓ of the rice, then a layer of fish and some gravy. Add a little of the fried onion, soaked saffron and chopped cilantro. Repeat the process again and finish with rice on top. Garnish with fried onions.
7. Cover the pan with foil, then the lid, and bake in a preheated 350°F (175°C) oven for 30 minutes.

Serves 8

Fish Cutlets

I have found that, if you use cans of tuna in oil, the cutlets turn out to be extremely greasy. Light tuna in water is a healthier, tasty alternative. If you wish to spice it up, add more ginger.

1. Boil the potatoes until tender and then mash.
2. Drain water from the tuna. Add the tuna to the potatoes with the ginger, garlic, salt and chili powder.
3. Add the chopped cilantro. Mix well together.
4. Form into cutlets, dip in egg then breadcrumbs and fry in a shallow pan on medium high heat until golden brown.

Serve with lemon slices, a salad and either parathas or chapatis. These can also be served with Tamarind Chutney (page 94) or Red Chili Chutney (page 96).

Serves 6

4	large potatoes	4
1	can water-packed tuna (8 oz./225 mL)	1
1 ½ tsp.	ginger (crushed)	7.5 mL
1 ½ tsp.	garlic (crushed)	7.5 mL
½ tsp.	salt	2.5 mL
½ tsp.	chili powder	2.5 mL
¼ cup	cilantro (chopped)	60 mL
1	egg (beaten)	1
1 ½ cups	breadcrumbs	360 mL

Fish Paka (Fish in Coconut Sauce)

Ingredients for fish:

3 lbs.	halibut or sole	1.35 kg
2 Tbsp.	fresh lemon juice	30 mL
1 tsp.	salt	5 mL
1/4 tsp.	chili powder	1.2 mL
1	large lemon (juice of)	1
1/2 tsp.	haldi (turmeric)	2.5 mL

Ingredients for curry:

1 3/4 cups	coconut milk	420 mL
1 tsp.	chili powder	5 mL
1/2 tsp.	garlic (crushed)	2.5 mL
1/2 tsp.	salt	2.5 mL
1/2 tsp.	haldi (turmeric)	2.5 mL
1/4 cup	fresh lemon juice	60 mL
1/2 tsp.	garam masala	2.5 mL
1/2 cup	water	120 mL
1	sprig of cilantro (chopped)	1

Fish Paka has a rich yellow texture with a tangy, distinctly coconut taste. So for all the seafood lovers out there, I guarantee this spicy coconut fish dish will become a favorite.

Method for fish:

1. Marinate the fish in the 2 Tbsp. (30 mL) lemon juice and salt for 30 minutes then wash it and pat dry.
2. Mix together the chili powder, remaining lemon juice and turmeric and smear over fish.
3. Bake in the oven at 400°F (200°C) for 25 minutes, or until done (fish will flake when touched with a fork).
4. Prepare the basic fish curry (below) while the fish is cooking.

Method for curry:

1. Pour the coconut milk into a large saucepan.
2. Add the chili powder, garlic, salt, turmeric and lemon juice and bring to a boil, stirring continuously for 3 minutes.
3. Add the garam masala and cook for 1 minute. Add the water and switch off the stove.
4. Pour over the baked fish before serving and garnish with chopped cilantro.

Serve with parathas or naan.

Serves 5

Fish Rolls

This is a lovely spring dish. It can be served as a wonderful light luncheon all by itself, or as a great start to a large dinner party.

Method for fish mixture:

1. Using 2 Tbsp. (30 mL) of oil, sauté the green onions on medium high heat until transparent.
2. Add the spinach, salt, pepper and green chilies and stir well.
3. Add the shredded fish and lemon juice.
4. Cook for 5 minutes, stirring gently. Add cheese and remove from heat.

Method for batter:

1. Mix together the flour, 1 beaten egg, water, salt and green chili to make the pancakes.
2. Spoon 2 Tbsp. (30 mL) of the fish mixture onto each pancake and roll it up.
3. Dip into beaten egg.
4. In a frying pan, on medium high heat, fry each pancake in about 1 tsp. (5 mL) of oil until golden brown.

Serve with leaf lettuce and thinly sliced cucumber.

Serves 6–8

Ingredients for fish mixture:

2 Tbsp.	vegetable oil	30 mL
1 Tbsp.	green onions	15 mL
2 oz.	boiled spinach	57 g
1 tsp.	salt	5 mL
½ tsp.	black pepper	2.5 mL
2	green chilies (chopped)	2
1 lb.	fish (boiled and shredded —see note below)	455 g
1 Tbsp.	fresh lemon juice	15 mL
1 Tbsp.	cheese, shredded (cheddar)	15 mL

Ingredients for batter:

1 ½ cups	all-purpose flour	560 mL
1	egg (beaten)	1
1 cup	water	240 mL
1 tsp.	salt	5 mL
1	green chili (chopped)	1
1	egg for cooking pancakes (beaten)	1
	vegetable oil for frying	

 In this dish you can use any kind of fish. I alternate between halibut, salmon and snapper.

Masala Fish

This spicy coconut fish dish is guaranteed to become a favorite seafood recipe.

Ingredients for fish:

1 ½ lbs.	halibut	700 g
1 Tbsp.	salt	15 mL
2 Tbsp.	fresh lemon juice	30 mL
1	green chili	1
1	bunch of cilantro	1
¼ tsp.	salt	1.2 mL
¼ tsp.	chili powder	1.2 mL
1 Tbsp.	desiccated coconut	15 mL
3	sprigs of limro (curry leaves)	3
1 Tbsp.	whole dhania (coriander seeds)	15 mL
1 ½ tsp.	curry powder	7.5 mL
¼ cup	fresh lemon juice	60 mL

Ingredients for curry:

¼ cup	vegetable oil	60 mL
3	tomatoes (chopped)	3
½ tsp.	garlic (crushed)	2.5 mL
1 tsp.	curry powder	5 mL
¼ tsp.	jeera (ground cumin)	1.2 mL
1 tsp.	chili powder	5 mL
1 tsp.	tomato purée	5 mL
½ cup	fried onions	120 mL
½ cup	water	120 mL
¼ cup	chopped cilantro	60 mL

Method for fish:

1. Marinate the fish in 1 Tbsp. (15 mL) of salt and 2 Tbsp. (30 mL) lemon juice for 30 minutes.
2. Deseed the green chili. (Remember to oil your hands before handling it in order to protect your hands from burning.) Make a paste with the chili and remaining ingredients.
3. Wipe the salty moisture from the fish and smear with the paste.
4. Bake in oven at 400°F (200°C) for 20–25 minutes.
5. While the fish is cooking, prepare the basic fish curry as below.

Method for curry:

1. Heat the vegetable oil on medium high heat. Fry the chopped tomatoes and add the garlic, curry powder, ground cumin, chili powder and tomato purée. Add the fried onions and water.
2. Cover pan and leave to simmer until it becomes a thick gravy (about 3 minutes).
3. Pour over the baked fish before serving and garnish with chopped cilantro.

Serve with rice.

Serves 5

Fish Biriyani (p. 78) with Onion Salad (p. 103)

Clockwise from top: Navrattan Pilau (p. 128),
Aloo Gobi (p. 28) and Smokey Chicken Rice (p. 124)

Top: Chicken Corn Bake (p. 65)
bottom: Chicken with Peanut Butter (p. 57)

Clockwise from top: Masala Fish (p. 82), Fish Paka (p. 80) and Hot Prawn Curry (p. 86),

Oven-Baked Fish

Use fresh fish to make this dish, if possible, as it has much more flavor than with frozen fish. If you find it too spicy, the addition of Raita (see page 95) will help to soften the flavor.

3 lbs.	halibut or fillet of sole	1.35 kg
1 tsp.	each of salt and chili powder (or to taste)	5 mL
3	lemons (juice of)	3
½ tsp.	ground peppercorns	2.5 mL
1 tsp.	garlic (crushed)	5 mL
1 tsp.	oregano	5 mL
3 Tbsp.	vegetable oil	45 mL
2	medium tomatoes (puréed)	2
1	sprig of cilantro (finely chopped)	1

1. Wash the fish, salt it and pour lemon juice on it. Set aside for 1 hour.
2. Wash fish again, place in a glass dish and gently rub with the ground peppercorns and ½ tsp. (2.5 mL) of the garlic.
3. In a small saucepan, combine the remaining garlic, oregano, vegetable oil, tomatoes and cilantro and cook on low heat until evenly blended.
4. Pour the mixture over the fish and bake in the oven (preheated to 440°F/220°C) for 25 minutes or until fish flakes easily.

Serve with your choice of rice or naan.

Serves 4

Spicy Halibut Steaks

	oil for grilling	
¼ tsp.	jeera (cumin seeds) (coarsely crushed)	1.2 mL
½ cup	margarine or butter (melted)	120 mL
1 tsp.	salt	5 mL
2 tsp.	fresh lemon juice	10 mL
1 tsp.	prepared spicy mustard	5 mL
1 tsp.	chili powder	5 mL
3 lbs.	halibut or other lean fish steaks, each ³⁄₄ inch (1.8 cm) thick	1.35 kg

*T*his dish originates from the southwestern coastal state of Kerala, where the rivers are home to a diverse number of freshwater fish.

1. Grease the grill plate lightly.
2. Mix together all the ingredients except for the fish steaks. Brush the fish with this marinade.
3. Grill the fish for 6–8 minutes on each side, brushing frequently with the marinade, until the fish flakes easily with a fork.
4. Garnish with wedges of lemon and chopped fresh parsley if desired.

Serve with Potato Parathas (page 118).

Serves 4

Moghlai-Style Baked Lobster or Fish

I learned this technique last summer when I was at my sister's place. In the last few months, I have introduced it to many of my cousins who have responded with rave reviews. Here's hoping you like it too.

1. Prepare a cheese sauce. In a saucepan, melt ¼ cup (60 mL) of the butter on medium high heat, add flour and fry for 3 minutes.

2. Add ¾ tsp. (3.75 mL) of the salt and milk, and stir constantly until the sauce starts to thicken.

3. Now add half of the shredded cheese and continue stirring until the cheese blends in and the sauce becomes thick and creamy. Set aside.

4. In another saucepan, boil the lobster or fish in just enough water to cover it, plus the remaining ¾ tsp. (3.75 mL) salt, green chilies and vinegar. Boil for 10–12 minutes.

5. When the lobster or fish is tender, remove from saucepan and place in a glass ovenproof dish. Add Tabasco or chili sauce, sprinkle remaining cheese and ¼ cup (60 mL) butter cut into pieces over top, and broil for 10–12 minutes.

6. Pour sauce over top, and around the sides. Broil for another couple of minutes.

Serve hot with plain rice.

Serves 3

½ cup	butter	120 mL
1 cup	all-purpose flour	240 mL
1 ½ tsp.	salt	7.5 mL
4 cups	milk	950 mL
1 ½ cups	shredded cheddar or mozzarella cheese	360 mL
1 ½ lbs.	lobster or fish fillet (cut in small pieces)	700 g
½ tsp.	green chilies (finely chopped)	2.5 mL
1 Tbsp.	white vinegar	15 mL
1 tsp.	Tabasco or chili sauce	5 mL

Hot Prawn Curry

2 Tbsp.	ghee or oil	30 mL
1	medium onion (thinly sliced)	1
1 tsp.	garlic paste	5 mL
½ inch	piece ginger (cut into strips)	1.2 cm
1–2	bay leaves	1–2
1 tsp.	chili powder	5 mL
1 tsp.	curry powder	5 mL
1 tsp.	salt	5 mL
2 tsp.	tomato purée	10 mL
1 tsp.	black pepper	5 mL
1 cup	yogurt	240 mL
1 tsp.	garam masala	5 mL
1 cup	coconut milk (may use canned milk)	240 mL
2 lbs.	prawns (fresh or frozen)	900 g
½	bunch of cilantro (for garnish)	½

*T*he combination of ground and fresh spices makes this a very fragrant and delicious dish. It comes from the west coast of India where fresh seafood is abundant.

1. Heat the ghee or oil on medium heat in a saucepan. Add the onion and garlic paste, and fry gently until golden brown.
2. Add the ginger, bay leaves, chili powder, curry powder, salt, tomato purée, black pepper, yogurt, garam masala and coconut milk.
3. Stir continuously and let it boil for 5 minutes.
4. Add prawns and stir gently for 5 minutes or more.
5. Stir in cilantro and serve.

Serve with parathas and any green salad.

Serves 6–7

Prawns Hara (Green Prawns)

A much fancier version of curried prawns. Try it—you will love the results.

1. Heat the oil in a pan over medium heat.
2. Add the garlic, white part of the green onions, ginger, cumin, green chilies and turmeric powder. Cook for 1 minute.
3. Add the prawns and cook for five minutes then add the cilantro, spinach, mint and salt to taste. Stir for 5 minutes or more.
4. Before serving, add garam masala.

Serve with a rice dish or parathas.

Serves 3–4

3 Tbsp.	vegetable oil	45 mL
5–6	cloves garlic (chopped)	5–6
1	bunch of green onions, white parts only	1
2 Tbsp.	ginger (chopped)	30 mL
1 tsp.	jeera (cumin seeds)	5 mL
3 Tbsp.	green chilies (chopped)	45 mL
1/2 tsp.	haldi (turmeric powder)	2.5 mL
16	medium prawns (shelled and deveined)	16
2 Tbsp.	cilantro (chopped)	30 mL
1/2 lb.	spinach (chopped)	225 g
2 Tbsp.	mint (chopped)	30 mL
	salt to taste	
1 tsp.	garam masala	5 mL

Prawns in Chili Sauce

My family particularly enjoys this dish on a cold winter night.

Ingredients for prawns:

3 lbs.	tiger prawns	1.35 kg
½ tsp.	salt	2.5 mL
¼ cup	fresh lemon juice	60 mL
½ tsp.	garlic paste	2.5 mL
½ tsp.	chili powder	2.5 mL
3 Tbsp.	vegetable oil	45 mL

Ingredients for sauce:

1 tsp.	garlic paste	5 mL
1 ½ tsp.	salt	7.5 mL
½ tsp.	ground peppercorns	2.5 mL
¼ cup	fresh lemon juice	60 mL
1 ½ tsp.	chili powder	7.5 mL
¼ cup	water	60 mL

Method for prawns:

1. Shell and wash the prawns. Combine with the salt, lemon juice, garlic paste and chili powder.
2. Pour the vegetable oil in a frying pan on medium high heat. Fry the prawns for 2 minutes until cooked. When the prawns start turning red in color, you know they are cooked.

Method for sauce:

1. Use saucepan on medium heat and add the garlic paste, salt, ground peppercorns, lemon juice, chili powder and water. Cook until the sauce becomes thick, stirring constantly.
2. Spread the prawns on a dish and pour the sauce over.

Serve with naan and lemon slices on the side.

Serves 5

Chutneys, Pickles and Salads

Chutneys, raitas and salads play an important role in East Indian cuisine. Some salads provide a wholesome snack; others help perk up the main course. Most of the salads and chutneys are so delicious that they can be eaten on their own with any of the Indian breads like puris, naans or chapatis.

Many salads and chutneys are freshly made for each meal, but there are some like the Mango, Apple and Tamarind Chutneys that can be prepared ahead of time and taste even better! In fact, the quickest snack anyone could whip up for the unexpected visitor is chutney or pickles served with parathas or rotis—or even a slice of bread.

I hope you will enjoy these salads and chutneys with your special meals.

Apple Chutney

8	large apples	8
3	large onions (chopped)	3
1 cup	white vinegar	240 mL
¼ cup	sugar	60 mL
1 tsp.	salt	5 mL
3	cloves garlic	3
1 inch	piece ginger (crushed)	2.5 cm
1 tsp.	red chili powder	15 mL
1 tsp.	jeera (cumin powder)	5 mL
1 cup	fresh lemon juice	240 mL
1 cup	apple juice	240 mL

 This chutney is good for 2 weeks if refrigerated.

This East Indian chutney is used as a condiment with rice and curry.

1. Peel, core and grate apples into a pot.
2. Add the chopped onions.
3. Add the vinegar, sugar, salt, spices and lemon juice.
4. Cook for 1 hour on low heat until thick.
5. Add the apple juice and cook on low heat for 10 minutes, stirring constantly.
6. Cool and store in a glass jar.
7. Serve cool.

Serve with Samosas (see pages 24–26), Dahi Kebabs (see page 20) or any other appetizer of your choice.

Makes 2 large bowls of chutney

Coconut Chutney

1	bunch of cilantro	1
2	green chilies (hot)	2
½ cup	desiccated coconut	120 mL
½ tsp.	salt	2.5 mL
2 Tbsp.	fresh lemon juice	30 mL

 This chutney keeps for 1 week if refrigerated.

An East Indian chutney served mainly with pakoras, bhajiyas and kebabs. Can also be served with pilau rice.

1. Wash and chop the cilantro and green chilies.
2. Blend all the ingredients together until a smooth consistency is achieved.
3. Refrigerate and serve when required.

Makes 1 large bowl of chutney

Dhania Chutney

1. Wash and chop the cilantro, green onions and green chilies.
2. Purée in a food processor or blender.
3. Add the salt, sugar and cumin seeds.
4. Purée for 20 more seconds.
5. Add the lemon juice and refrigerate.

Makes 1 large bowl of chutney

1	bunch of cilantro	1
1	bunch of green onions	1
2	green chilies (hot) (deseeded)	2
½ tsp.	salt	2.5 mL
2 tsp.	sugar	10 mL
1 tsp.	jeera (cumin seeds, roasted)	5 mL
2 Tbsp.	fresh lemon juice	30 mL

This chutney is good for 1 week if refrigerated.

Cumin seeds can be roasted dry on a frying pan on low heat for about 6 minutes, stirring continuously or until the color changes to a light brown shade. They can be stored in an airtight jar for future use.

Khajur Chutney

1 cup	khajur (dates)	240 mL
1 cup	sugar	240 mL
1 cup	fresh lemon juice	240 mL
1 Tbsp.	jeera (cumin) (coarsely ground)	15 mL
½ cup	mint	120 mL
½ cup	green chilies (approximately 6)	120 mL

 This chutney keeps for 10 days if refrigerated.

A delectable date chutney—the favorite of many people in Zanzibar, the tropical spice island off the coast of East Africa.

1. Cut dates very fine.
2. In a bowl mix the dates, sugar and lemon juice.
3. Chop the mint and green chilies finely.
4. Mix everything together and let sit for 2–3 days.
5. Store in a glass jar and serve as a condiment.

Serve with Shami Kebabs (see page 22).

Makes 1 large bowl of chutney

Podina Chutney

2	large bunches of mint leaves	2
1	bunch of cilantro	1
1	bunch of green onions	1
2	green chilies (hot)	2
½ tsp.	salt	2.5 mL
2 tsp.	sugar	10 mL
2 Tbsp.	fresh lemon juice	30 mL
4 Tbsp.	water	60 mL

This chutney keeps for 1 week if refrigerated.

This mouthwatering chutney is extremely popular all over India, especially when served with a variety of vegetarian snacks.

1. Wash and chop the cilantro, green onions and green chilies.
2. Blend to a smooth purée.
3. Add the salt, sugar, lemon juice and water.
4. Purée for 20 more seconds.
5. Refrigerate and serve when required.

Serve with Vegetable Samosas (see page 26).

Makes 1 large bowl of chutney

Sweet Mango Chutney

Fresh, tangy and easy to make, this chutney goes well with all dishes.

1. Mix together the mango cubes and sugar in a pot. Keep covered for 24 hours.
2. Remove the mango cubes from the sugar (but keep the mango aside) and boil the sugar until sticky (approximately 10 minutes). Let cool.
3. When cool, add the mango and all the other ingredients.
4. Serve cool. Store in the refrigerator.

Serve with Spinach Kebabs (see page 18).

Makes 1 large bowl of chutney

1 lb.	mango (raw and cut in cubes)	455 g
³/₄ lb.	sugar	340 g
¹/₂ cup	chili powder	120 mL
¹/₂ cup	dhania (coriander seeds) (coarsely ground)	120 mL
¹/₂ cup	rai (black mustard seeds)	120 mL
¹/₄ cup	methi (fenugreek)	60 mL
1 Tbsp.	salt	15 mL

This chutney keeps for 5 days if refrigerated.

*When boiling in step 2, **do not** add water because it will spoil the chutney.*

Tamarind Chutney

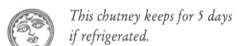

¼ lb.	tamarind (see page 68)	113 g
2 cups	water	475 mL
1 tsp.	salt	5 mL
3 Tbsp.	sugar	45 mL
1 Tbsp.	jeera (cumin powder)	15 mL
2 Tbsp.	chili powder	30 mL
2 Tbsp.	carrot (finely grated)	30 mL

This chutney keeps for 5 days if refrigerated.

*T*his very tangy chutney makes a great dipping sauce too.

1. Soak tamarind in water overnight.
2. Remove seeds and blend. Strain into a saucepan.
3. Add the salt, sugar and cumin powder and simmer for 15 minutes.
4. Add the chili powder and carrot. Cook for 5 minutes.
5. Remove from heat and cool before serving.
6. Store in the refrigerator.

Serve with Shami Kebabs (page 22) or any meat appetizers.

Makes 1 large bowl of chutney

Vinegar Chili Chutney

3 cups	white vinegar	720 mL
2 cups	sugar	475 mL
½ cup	chili powder	120 mL
½ cup	tomato paste	120 mL

Will keep well in the refrigerator for about 2 weeks.

A tasty chutney with the hot, spicy, tang of vinegar.

1. Mix together the vinegar, sugar and chili powder in a pot.
2. Boil until it forms a thick, sticky syrup (about 5 minutes).
3. Add the tomato paste.
4. Continue to boil for 3–5 minutes.
5. Cool before serving.
6. Store in the refrigerator.

Serve with Vegetable Kebabs (see page 19).

Makes 1 large bowl of chutney

Raita

Raita is a very popular Indian relish. It is prepared with yogurt and lots of herbs and spices to give it a special spicy Indian aroma.

1. Mix all the ingredients into the yogurt.
2. Chill before serving.

Raita goes very well with rice, tandoori and vegetable dishes, as well as with many appetizers, such as samosas and pakoras.

Makes 2 large bowls

2 cups	yogurt	475 mL
1	small cucumber (finely chopped)	1
2–3	green chilies (finely chopped)	2–3
1	small onion (finely chopped)	1
2	sprigs each of cilantro and mint leaves (finely chopped)	2
½ tsp.	salt	2.5 mL
½ tsp.	ground black pepper	2.5 mL
1 tsp.	sugar	5 mL
2 Tbsp.	fresh lemon juice	30 mL

 This keeps well for 2 days if refrigerated.

Chutneys, Pickles and Salads

Red Chili Chutney

Hot, spicy chutney that will set your palate on fire. If you are bold and daring, try this chutney to give your meal that extra kick.

2 cups	white vinegar	475 mL
2 cups	sugar	475 mL
¼ lb.	red dried chilies (Kashmiri chilies)	113 g
3 Tbsp.	garlic (crushed)	45 mL

1. Mix the vinegar and sugar together in a pot.
2. Boil until sticky (about 5 minutes).
3. Blend the chilies and garlic together.
4. Add the chili/garlic mixture to the boiled vinegar.
5. Boil again for a few minutes.
6. Cool before serving.
7. Store in the refrigerator.

Serve with Dhokra (page 16).

Makes 1 large bowl of chutney

 This will keep for a couple of weeks in the refrigerator.

Carrot Pickles

A very popular side dish for pilaus or curry. This pickle is so delicious that it can even be eaten on its own with naan or roti.

1	large carrot	1
1 Tbsp.	tomato paste	15 mL
¼ tsp.	garlic (crushed)	1.2 mL
¼ tsp.	sugar	1.2 mL
2 tsp.	fresh lemon juice	10 mL
¼ tsp.	haldi (turmeric)	1.2 mL
1 ½ tsp.	cilantro (chopped)	7.5 mL

1. Peel, wash and grate the carrot.
2. Put in a bowl and add the rest of the ingredients. Mix well.
3. Chill in the refrigerator for 20 minutes.

Server cold as a condiment with any meal or appetizer.

Serves 3

 This is good for 2 days if refrigerated.

Beetroot Salad

This salad is mostly served with snacks like pizza, rotis, and parathas.

1. Heat the vegetable oil and add the cumin, mustard seeds, red chilies and curry leaves. Cover until the seeds have popped.
2. Let cool, and then add the beetroot and potato.
3. Mix the yogurt with salt and sugar and pour over the beetroot mixture.
4. Garnish with chopped cilantro.

Serve cold.

Serves 6

1 Tbsp.	vegetable oil	15 mL
1 tsp.	jeera (cumin) (crushed)	5 mL
1 1/2 tsp.	rai (black mustard seeds)	7.5 mL
4	red chilies (whole and dried)	4
4–5	limro (fresh curry leaves)	4–5
1	beetroot (boiled and cut into small pieces)	1
1	potato (boiled, peeled and cut into small pieces)	1
2 cups	yogurt	475 mL
1/2 tsp.	salt	2.5 mL
1/2 tsp.	sugar	2.5 mL
1/4 cup	cilantro (chopped)	60 mL

Coconut Rice Salad

This salad is generally served with barbecued meals.

1. Cook the rice and allow to cool.
2. Mix with the other ingredients in a large bowl.
3. Chill and serve cold.

Serves 4

1/2 cup	rice	120 mL
1 cup	water	240 mL
1/2 cup	English cucumber (chopped)	120 mL
1/2 cup	parsley (chopped)	120 mL
1/2 cup	tomatoes (chopped)	120 mL
1/4 cup	nuts (chopped —your preference)	60 mL
2 Tbsp.	coconut cream	30 mL

Corn Salad

ostly served with barbecued meats. Bet you would never have thought of this!

Ingredients for dressing:

1 tsp.	sugar or honey	5 mL
1 cup	yogurt	240 mL
½ cup	mayonnaise	120 mL
½ tsp.	salt	2.5 mL
½ tsp.	ground black pepper	2.5 mL

Ingredients for salad:

2 ½ cups	corn kernels (boiled)	600 mL
1 cup	carrot (diced)	240 mL
1 cup	English cucumber (diced)	240 mL
1 cup	tomatoes (diced)	240 mL
1 ½ cups	cauliflower (cut in small pieces)	360 mL
1	apple (diced)	1

1. Prepare the dressing by combining all the ingredients in a small bowl.
2. Put the vegetables into a large bowl.
3. Pour the dressing into the main ingredients, and toss.
4. Chill and serve cold.

Serves 6

 This salad is good for 2 days if refrigerated.

Dried Fruit and Rice Salad

There are endless ways of serving this salad. Try it as an appetizer with grilled meat or with naan and curry.

1. Prepare the dressing by mixing together the dressing ingredients in a large bowl.
2. Toast the pine nuts and sunflower seeds in a dry frying pan for 5 minutes or until they turn light brown in color. Add them to the other salad ingredients and toss well to cover evenly.
3. Chill and serve cold.

Serves 6

Ingredients for dressing:

2 Tbsp.	vegetable oil	30 mL
1/2 cup	orange juice	120 mL
1/2 tsp.	garlic (crushed)	2.5 mL
1/2 tsp.	ginger (grated)	2.5 mL
2 tsp.	honey	10 mL
1 Tbsp.	white vinegar	15 mL
1 Tbsp.	fresh lemon juice	15 mL
1 tsp.	chili powder (optional)	5 mL

Ingredients for salad:

1/4 cup	pine nuts (toasted)	60 mL
1/4 cup	sunflower seeds (toasted)	60 mL
1 cup	rice boiled with 1 1/2 cups (360 mL) water and cooled	240 mL
1/2 cup	sultanas or other raisins	120 mL
2	apricots (peeled and chopped)	2
2 Tbsp.	ginger (peeled and chopped)	30 mL
2	dried prunes (pitted and chopped)	2
1	celery stick (chopped)	1
1/2 cup	green onions (chopped)	120 mL
1/2 cup	each red and green bell pepper (chopped)	120 mL

Fresh Vegetable Salad

Ingredients for dressing:

2 cups	yogurt	475 mL
1 Tbsp.	sugar	15 mL
1 tsp.	salt	5 mL
½ cup	green mint	120 mL
1 tsp.	ground black pepper	5 mL
1 tsp.	jeera (cumin) (crushed)	5 mL
½ tsp.	salt	2.5 mL

Ingredients for salad:

2	medium carrots (peeled and diced)	2
1	medium cucumber (peeled and diced)	1
1	medium tomato (chopped)	1
½	bunch of green onions (chopped finely)	½
½ cup	French beans (diced)	120 mL
1 cup	corn kernels (boiled)	240 mL
½ cup	green pepper (chopped)	120 mL
½ cup	mushrooms (chopped)	120 mL
2 cups	lettuce leaves (shredded)	475 mL
1 cup	radish (chopped)	240 mL

This salad is served in most Indian homes. You can serve it as an accompaniment to rice and curry, but it also goes well with any main meal.

1. Combine all the dressing ingredients in a large bowl.
2. Add the salad ingredients to the dressing mixture. Toss well.
3. Chill and serve cold.

Serves 6

Indian-Style Potato Salad

A light salad and a perfect party food. This can be prepared ahead of time.

1. Boil and peel potatoes, then cut into small cubes.
2. Heat the vegetable oil to a medium high heat then add the cumin, mustard, red chilies and curry leaves and cover the pot immediately, cooking for 30 seconds.
3. Add the potatoes.
4. Add yogurt and mix well.
5. Stir in the salt and sugar and sprinkle with chopped cilantro.
6. Remove from heat.

Serve cold.

Serves 5

2 lbs.	potatoes	900 g
1 Tbsp.	vegetable oil	15 mL
1 tsp.	jeera (cumin seeds) (whole)	5 mL
1 tsp.	rai (black mustard seeds) (whole)	5 mL
3–4	red chilies (whole)	3–4
3–4	limro (fresh curry leaves)	3–4
2 cups	yogurt	475 mL
1 tsp.	salt	5 mL
1 tsp.	sugar	5 mL
½	bunch of cilantro (chopped)	½

Kachumber (Indian Mixed Salad)

A typical East Indian salad, usually served with pilau rice.

1. Thinly slice onion into rings.
2. Cut the green chili into thin rings.
3. Chop the carrot, radish and cilantro.
4. Mix vegetables in a large bowl.
5. Add the vinegar and crushed garlic to the mixture.
6. Add the salt and red chili powder (if using).

Serves 4

1	medium onion	1
1	green chili	1
1	medium carrot	1
1	medium radish	1
1	sprig of cilantro	1
2 Tbsp.	white vinegar	30 mL
¼ tsp.	garlic (crushed)	1.2 mL
¼ tsp.	salt (optional)	1.2 mL
¼ tsp.	red chili powder (optional)	1.2 mL

Mixed Vegetable and Fruit Salad

*S*erve this rich tasting salad in a small portion as an appetizer or as a side dish for a picnic.

2	potatoes	2
½ cup	green pepper (chopped)	120 mL
2 cups	mixed vegetables (peas, carrots, corn—frozen vegetable mix may be used)	475 mL
1	medium English cucumber	1
½ cup	mushrooms (chopped)	120 mL
½	bunch of green onions	½
1	apple (cut in small pieces)	1
10	whole seedless green grapes	10

Ingredients for dressing:

1 cup	milk	240 mL
½ cup	mayonnaise (low-fat can be used)	120 mL
½ tsp.	salt	2.5 mL
1 tsp.	sugar or honey	5 mL
½ tsp.	black pepper (crushed)	2.5 mL

1. Cube the potatoes, chop the green pepper and boil with the 2 cups (475 mL) mixed vegetables.
2. Chop the cucumber, mushrooms and green onions and add to the other vegetables.
3. Mix together the dressing ingredients until creamy.
4. Mix the dressing with the vegetables.
5. Add the apple pieces and grapes.
6. Chill and serve cold.

Serves 6

Onion Salad

Fresh, tangy and quick to make, this salad complements all dishes.

1. Slice onions very thinly and put into a bowl.
2. Add the chopped mint leaves and celery seeds.
3. Cut the green chilies in very thin rings and add to the above mixture with the salt.
4. Just before serving add the sliced tomatoes and vinegar and toss.

Serve with any dish of your choice.

Serves 4–5

1	large sweet red onion	1
2	large sweet white onions	2
1 Tbsp.	chopped fresh mint leaves	15 mL
1 tsp.	celery seeds	5 mL
2	green chilies (deseeded)	2
¼ tsp.	salt	1.2 mL
1	medium tomato (sliced)	1
½ cup	white vinegar	120 mL

Red Kidney Bean Salad

Ingredients for dressing:

1/2 cup	white vinegar	120 mL
1/4 cup	salad or olive oil	60 mL
1/2 tsp.	garlic (crushed)	2.5 mL
1 tsp.	salt	5 mL
2 tsp.	sugar	10 mL
1 tsp.	chili powder	5 mL

Ingredients for salad:

3 cups	red kidney beans (or 3 cans, 7 oz./200 mL each)	600 mL
1	small onion (finely chopped)	1
2	green onions (chopped)	2
2	tomatoes (chopped)	2
1	cucumber (finely chopped)	1
1	green chili (finely chopped)	1

*S*erve this rich salad with any of your favorite appetizers. I like serving it with Samosas (see pages 24–26) or Fish Cutlets (see page 79).

1. Combine the dressing ingredients in a large bowl.
2. Add salad ingredients to the dressing and toss.
3. Chill for 1 hour and serve cold.

Serves 6

Breads, Puris and Rotis

Traditionally we serve curries and other main dishes with either rotis (chapatis), parathas or naans. In this chapter we introduce a variety of East Indian breads, from everyday rotis and puris to elaborate naans and parathas (and stuffed rotis).

Rotis are very easy to make and appeal to most people. In northern and central India, wheat is the most popular grain and consequently people eat rotis in preference to rice. Though makki (maize), jowel (millet), bajra (milo), daals (lentils) and even rice are used to make some forms of roti, most rotis are made of whole-wheat flour (atta) and are cooked in a heated Tawa or skillet.

Parathas are richer, softer and flakier than rotis and have a longer preparation time. They can be spiced before shallow-frying.

Naans are traditionally baked in a tandoor, or clay oven, but can also be done on the electric stove and baked in the oven.

Puris are a very popular bread for festive occasions and can be prepared in advance or frozen for later use.

Bhaturas are Punjabi-style leavened puris that use approximately two parts of white flour and one part of semolina (ground durum wheat flour).

Use your imagination to create new combinations of meals and breads.

Bhaturas

2 cups	all-purpose flour	475 mL
1 cup	semolina	240 mL
¼ tsp.	baking soda	1.2 mL
½ tsp.	baking powder	2.5 mL
½ tsp.	salt	2.5 mL
2 Tbsp.	yogurt	30 mL
2 tsp.	sugar	10 mL
2 cups	vegetable oil	475 mL

*B*haturas are a very tasty flat, deep-fried bread commonly served hot with curry. I recommend serving them with mouth-watering Punjabi Chole (page 48). Bhaturas can either be deep-fried or baked in a hot oven at 450°F (235°C), lightly brushed with oil first. Baking them will not puff them up as will deep-frying.*

1. Sieve the flour into a bowl and then add the semolina to it.
2. Add the baking soda, baking powder and salt.
3. Add the yogurt and sugar and mix gently. When fully mixed, knead together with enough water (1 ½–2 cups/360–475 mL) to make a soft pliable dough.
4. Cover with a moistened cloth and set aside for approximately 1 hour.
5. Divide the dough into 10–12 equal parts, shape into balls and place them on a lightly greased surface.
6. Heat the vegetable oil to medium heat in a deep-frying pan.
7. Flatten each ball to about 5 inches in diameter between lightly oiled palms.
8. Deep-fry until golden brown, turning once to ensure the bread puffs up. It will take approximately 1 minute for each bhatura to cook.

Makes 10–12

Spinach Bread

*S*pinach Bread is a delightful savory bread served mainly as an appetizer. This would be a great starter to a nice Tandoori dinner, a little fussy but well worth the effort.

1. Sift the flour into a large bowl. Add the oil, salt and yeast and thoroughly mix in approximately 1 cup (240 mL) of water to make a firm dough. Cover and set aside to rise for about 3 hours.
2. Meanwhile, prepare the filling. Boil the spinach for 2 minutes then drain and put in cold water.
3. Melt the butter and sauté the chopped onions for 1 minute. Remove excess water from the spinach and add to the onions. Add the salt, pepper and cheese. Mix well and let cool.
4. When the dough is doubled in size, roll it into a rectangle shape and spread 1 Tbsp. (15 mL) butter on top. Fold the dough. Repeat twice. Roll once more but this time fold it without any butter. Cover and refrigerate for ½ hour.
5. Roll the dough into a rectangle again about ½ inch (2.5 cm) thick. Cut in 3 strips lenghwise and put some filling onto each strip. Fold dough lengthwise to seal in filling and twist the strips together into a loose braid.
6. Lay the braid on a greased baking tray. You may shape it round like a jelly roll or as you like. If you want smaller loaves you may cut the dough into two before shaping. Brush bread with the egg. Let double in size.
7. Bake in a preheated oven at 350°F (175°C) for 20–25 minutes (15–20 minutes for smaller loaves) until hollow and golden brown.
8. Carefully lift the bread from the baking tray and cool on a wire rack.

Makes 8

Ingredients for bread:

4 cups	all-purpose flour	950 mL
2 Tbsp.	vegetable oil	30 mL
2 tsp.	salt	10 mL
2 tsp.	instant yeast	10 mL
2 cups	water	475 mL
3 Tbsp.	butter, softened	45 mL

Ingredients for filling:

1 lb.	spinach (cleaned and chopped)	455 g
2 Tbsp.	butter	30 mL
1 cup	green onions (chopped)	240 mL
1 tsp.	salt	5 mL
1 tsp.	black pepper	5 mL
½ lb.	feta cheese	225 g
1	egg (beaten)	1

Helpful Hint:
To keep the bread warm, wrap it in a tea towel and then in newspapers. This way it will stay warm longer—the best way to take it for a picnic.

Rotis/Chapatis

2 cups	atta flour (chapati flour)	475 mL
3 Tbsp.	melted butter or ghee	45 mL
1 tsp.	salt	5 mL
2 cups	water	475 mL

This is the basic method for making the Indian flatbread known as rotis. If you double the quantity, they can be wrapped in a foil sheet and frozen for future meals or even served for breakfast with an omelet. This traditional bread has accompanied almost every meal in East Indian homes. It should be made 30 minutes before serving and complements any curry. As an alternative for a snack, my son Zuher enjoys eating rotis by laying them flat, sprinkling sugar on them, and rolling them into a burrito-like roll.

1. Mix the atta flour with 2 Tbsp. (30 mL) of the melted butter or ghee and salt.
2. Pour in the water and knead the dough until it becomes soft.
3. Cover the dough and set aside for 1 hour to rise.
4. After 1 hour knead the dough again and add a bit of ghee (1/4 tsp./1.2 mL).
5. Roll out the dough into small balls (size of golf balls).
6. Flatten each ball and sprinkle lightly on both sides with atta flour. Also sprinkle the work surface with flour.
7. Roll out the rotis until they are about 8 inches (20 cm) in diameter.
8. Dry cook on a hot frying pan or tawa (traditional pan used only for rotis).
9. Cook until slightly spotted on both sides.
10. When done, brush lightly with melted butter or ghee.

Makes 10

Simply Indian

Puris

Puris are central India's equivalent of the North's roti. These unleavened puffed breads are usually deep-fried. You can make your own variations by stuffing with vegetables, daals, or even ground beef. Put 1 tsp. (5 mL) of stuffing in the middle of the dough, then seal it up and deep-fry.

1 cup	all-purpose flour	240 mL
1/4 tsp.	salt	1.2 mL
1 Tbsp.	vegetable oil	15 mL
1/3 cup	water	80 mL
2 cups	vegetable oil for deep-frying	475 mL

1. Mix together the flour, salt and oil and rub until the mixture resembles breadcrumbs.
2. Form into a dough by adding water and kneading to make a soft pliable dough.
3. Divide dough into 10 portions. Form into small balls, the size of golf balls.
4. Roll out to about 1 1/2 inches (3.8 cm) in diameter.
5. Heat the 2 cups (475 mL) of oil in a pan to medium high. Fry about 3 at a time by tapping them with a spoon until they puff up and turn golden brown.

Serve with vegetable curry, for breakfast lunch or dinner.

Makes 10

Variation 1—Sooji Puris

Add the following to the basic recipe:

1 cup   sooji (cream of wheat)   240 mL

1. Add the cream of wheat to dry ingredients in step 1.
2. Follow from step 2 onward.

Variation 2—Farsee Puris

Add the following to the basic recipe:

1/4 tsp.	crushed peppercorns	2.5 mL
1 Tbsp.	crushed jeera (cumin)	15 mL
1/3 cup	milk	80 mL

1. Add the peppercorns and cumin in step 1.
2. Use cold milk instead of water.
3. Follow from step 3 onward.

Variation 3—Til Puris

Add the following to the basic recipe:

2 tsp.	sugar	10 mL
2 tsp.	celery seeds	10 mL
2 tsp.	onion seeds	10 mL
2 Tbsp.	sesame seeds	30 mL

1. Add these to the flour in step 1.
2. Follow from step 2 onward.

Puran Puris

This also works well as a dessert and is an all-time favorite of my son Kazim.

Ingredients for puran filling:

2 cups	channa daal	475 mL
2 cups	milk	475 mL
3 cups	unsalted butter	720 mL
5	cardamom seeds (ground)	5
1 cup	milk powder	240 mL
2 1/2 cups	sugar	600 mL
1/2 tsp.	saffron	2.5 mL
1 cup	almond powder	240 mL
1/4 tsp.	yellow food coloring	1.2 mL

Ingredients for puri (dough):

1 cup	sooji (cream of wheat)	240 mL
1 cup	hot milk	240 mL
1 cup	all-purpose flour	240 mL
1/2 cup	vegetable oil	120 mL
1/2 tsp.	salt	2.5 mL
1/4 cup	ghee (for greasing pan)	60 mL
1/2 cup	melted ghee for basting	120 mL

 The almond powder used in this recipe can be found in almost all East Indian grocery stores and large food stores.

1. To make the filling, soak the daal overnight. Boil with the 2 cups (475 mL) milk. Cool and blend well.
2. Heat the butter in a nonstick pan. Add the cardamom and fry lightly. Add the blended daal and cook on medium heat until the liquid has evaporated and the daal is slightly brown in color. (About 15 minutes.)
3. Add the milk powder, sugar, saffron, almond powder and food coloring—this is the puran.
4. To make the dough, mix the cream of wheat and hot milk in a food processor until soft. Add the flour, oil and salt. Mix until dough is soft but not sticky.
5. Divide the dough into 10 golf ball-sized balls. Roll each ball into a very thin roti (9 inches/22.5 cm diameter), sprinkling flour if dough sticks on your work area. Cook dry in a frying pan (similar to making chapatis or rotis).
6. Grease a roti pan or cookie sheet with 1/4 cup (60 mL) ghee. Put one layer of roti in the pan. Pour over 1/4 of the puran filling and then a layer of roti. Repeat this process until all the rotis and puran are used up, making sure the puran is the final layer.
7. Pour 1/2 cup (120 mL) of melted ghee over the puran and bake in a preheated oven at 300°F (150°C) for about 30 minutes or until the top is slightly brown.
8. Remove from the oven and let cool. Cut into 20 squares.

Serves 6–8

Pani Puris

Here you make the puris from the basic recipe (see page 109) and then serve with the filling below. These puris are usually served for formal afternoon tea parties and garden parties.

1. For the pani, grind the coriander leaves, mint leaves and green chilies to a fine paste in a blender.
2. Mix in the lemon juice, asafoetida, salt and sugar. Add approximately 2 cups (475 mL) of water and boil. Refrigerate after cooling.
3. To assemble the pani puri, arrange all other ingredients on a plate and keep the pani in a deep pot.
4. Make a hole in the center of each puri and fill with the filling ingredients and chutneys.
5. Stir the pani. Dip the puri in it. As the puri fills with pani, pop immediately in your mouth.

Serves 4–6

Ingredients for pani (flavored water):

2 Tbsp.	cilantro	30 mL
1 cup	mint leaves	240 mL
2 Tbsp.	green chilies	30 mL
2	lemons (juice of)	2
1/4 tsp	asafoetida	1.2 mL
2 Tbsp.	salt	30 mL
1/4 tsp.	sugar	1.2 mL
2 cups	water	475 mL

Ingredients for filling:

16	puris (use puri recipe on page 109 but divide into 16 balls)	16
1/2 lb.	boiled potatoes (peeled and chopped)	225 g
1 Tbsp.	Dhania Chutney (see page 91)	15 mL
2 Tbsp.	Tamarind Chutney (see page 94)	30 mL
1/2 lb.	boiled channa (chickpeas)	225 g
1 cup	sprouted moong	240 mL

 Sprouted moong is found in most East Indian grocery stores and large food stores.

Masala Puris

1 1/2 cups	cake flour	360 mL
1/2 cup	channa or pea flour	120 mL
1/2 tsp.	salt	2.5 mL
1/2 cup	cilantro leaves	120 mL
4	green chilies	4
1 tsp.	garlic paste	5 mL
1 tsp.	mixed herbs	5 mL
1/4 tsp.	celery seeds	1.2 mL
2 Tbsp.	vegetable oil (for dough)	30 mL
3/4 cup	water	180 mL
4 cups	vegetable oil (for deep-frying)	950 mL

On an icy cold day, nothing warms you more than curling up on a comfy chair, watching your favorite movie and enjoying a serving of Masala Puri to accompany your daal. Even though the green chilies give these puris their zesty taste, reducing them to two, for all the mild spice lovers out there, will not lessen the flavor in any way.

1. Sieve together the cake flour, channa or pea flour and salt.
2. Pound the cilantro leaves, green chilies, garlic paste, mixed herbs and celery seeds together. Add this to the sieved ingredients.
3. Add the 2 Tbsp. (30 mL) vegetable oil and mix.
4. Add enough water to make the dough soft and pliable.
5. Set aside covered with a tea towel for 15 minutes to let the dough elasticize.
6. Divide into 10 equal parts about the size of golf balls.
7. Place the balls on a slightly floured surface and flatten with a rolling pin into circles of about 4 inches (10 cm) diameter.
8. Heat the remaining oil in a wok or deep frying pan to medium high.
9. Fry each puri until golden brown, turning once to ensure it puffs up.

Serve with Masoor Daal Curry (page 43).

Makes 10

Daal Puris (Stuffed Pea Rotis)

*P*uris are usually deep-fried, but in the case of Daal Puri *they are pan-fried. This is a personalized version of Puri that uses green chilies and onions. A definite family favorite and one you must try for yourself.*

1. To make the filling, boil peas in 2 cups (475 mL) water with salt, chili powder, cumin powder and garlic paste for 10–12 minutes. Reduce heat and simmer until peas are tender and the water has evaporated.
2. Using a food processor, grind pea mixture into a smooth paste with green chilies, coriander and green onion. Set aside.
3. To make the puris, mix together the flour, baking powder, salt, oil and water. Form a soft but not sticky dough.
4. Divide both the pea mixture and the dough into 10–12 balls each.
5. Roll out dough 3 inches (7.5 cm) round, brush with oil. Put a ball of pea mixture in the center, flatten and encase with dough.
6. Roll out to about 5 inches (12.5 cm) in diameter. Brush both sides with oil and cook in a nonstick frying pan until risen.

Serve with curry of your choice.

Makes 10–12

Ingredients for filling:

1 cup	yellow split peas (soaked overnight)	240 mL
2 cups	water	475 mL
1 tsp.	salt	5 mL
1/2 tsp.	chili powder	2.5 mL
1/2 tsp.	jeera (cumin powder)	2.5 mL
1/2 tsp.	garlic paste	2.5 mL
2	long green chilies (chopped)	2
2 Tbsp.	cilantro (chopped)	30 mL
1	green onion (finely chopped)	1

Ingredients for puri (dough):

2 cups	all-purpose flour	475 mL
1/4 tsp.	baking powder	1.2 mL
1/2 tsp.	salt	2.5 mL
1/4 cup	vegetable oil	60 mL
3/4 cup	water	180 mL
2 Tbsp.	vegetable oil (for brushing)	30 mL

Naan

2 ½ tsp.	instant yeast	12.5 mL
1 tsp.	sugar	5 mL
½ cup	warm water	120 mL
2 ½ cups	all-purpose flour	600 mL
1 tsp.	salt	5 mL
¼ cup	vegetable oil	60 mL
1	egg (beaten)	1
5 Tbsp.	milk powder	75 mL
5 Tbsp.	yogurt	75 mL
2 Tbsp.	melted butter	30 mL
2 Tbsp.	warm milk	30 mL
	sesame seeds (optional)	

Traditionally, naans are baked in clay ovens called tandoors, but this recipe uses a conventional oven and stove top. Naans originate from the Punjab and accompany tandoori meat dishes and vegetable tarkaris very well. They are also our favorite bread with Butter Chicken (see page 51)!

1. Mix together the yeast, sugar and warm water and let proof for 5 minutes.
2. Add the flour, salt, vegetable oil, beaten egg and milk powder and mix together.
3. Add the yogurt and gradually work into the mixture to form a soft pliable dough.
4. Knead vigorously and cover with a moistened tea towel. Leave in a warm place to rise to just less than double its size (about 2 hours).
5. Dust hands with plenty of flour and shape dough into 6 large balls.
6. Make these into oval pancakes by gently rolling them out and pulling the dough gently into a "tear" shape.
7. Brush top side with melted butter and the bottom side with milk and place in frying pan. If desired, scatter sesame seeds on top.
8. Broil each naan on high to cook the top part, then remove and cook on the stove to cook the bottom part. This will take a few minutes and once cooked the naan will slide easily out of the frying pan.

Makes 6

Simply Indian

Clockwise from top: Naan (p. 114), Potato Parathas (p. 118),
Rotis/Chapatis (p. 108), Bhaturas (p. 106), and Yeast Dahi Parathas (p. 120)

Masala Dosa (p. 46) with Lassi Drink (p. 155)

Clockwise from top: Green Pea Pilau (p. 122),
Coorgese Vegetable Pilau (p. 125),
and Punjabi Chole (p. 48)

bowl: Kheer (p. 148),
small platter: Monthal (p. 143), Badaam Paak (p. 134)

large platter, clockwise from bottom: Jalebi (p. 149), Pera (p. 141),
Mesoob (p. 146), Rasgullas (p. 137), Laddoo (p. 144), Barfi with edible silver and pistachio (p. 150)

Naan (Semi-Sweet Bread)

I was taught the simplicity of making this rich-textured bread in my teenage years, and it is still the most popular bread dish in and out of my classes. Many people assume naans are difficult to make, but they are quite simple. Naans can also be prepared ahead of time and frozen.

1. Sieve the flour and salt into a big bowl.
2. Make a hole in the center of the flour and add the sugar, lightly beaten egg, water, margarine, yeast, food coloring and milk powder and make a soft pliable dough. Cover and leave to rise in a warm place for 3 hours.
3. Divide the dough into 6 parts. Roll each part into a big circle 12 inches (30 cm) in diameter and 1 ½ inches (3.8 cm) thick.
4. Place in a large, round greased baking tray. Let rise again for one hour. Brush with beaten egg or evaporated milk and sprinkle with sesame seeds.
5. Bake in a preheated oven at 350°F (175°C) for 10–15 minutes.

Makes 6

4 cups	all-purpose flour	950 mL
½ tsp.	salt	2.5 mL
½ cup	sugar	120 mL
1	egg (lightly beaten)	1
1 ¾ cups	water	420 mL
2 Tbsp.	margarine	30 mL
2 tsp.	instant yeast	10 mL
	pinch of yellow food coloring	
3 Tbsp.	milk powder	45 mL
	beaten egg or evaporated milk for brushing	
2 tsp.	sesame seeds	10 mL

Mkate Kumimina (Sweet Rice Cake)

3 cups	basmati rice	720 mL
2 1/2 cups	coconut cream	600 mL
1 cup	milk	240 mL
2 cups	warm water	475 mL
2 tsp.	instant yeast	10 mL
1 Tbsp.	butter	15 mL
2 cups	sugar	475 mL
1 tsp.	cardamom seeds (crushed)	5 mL
2 Tbsp.	ghee or butter	30 mL

Mkate Kumimina originates from the island of Zanzibar, off the coast of East Africa. Filling, but not heavy, this dessert is flavored with cardamom seeds. My grandchildren enjoy it with a cup of Masala Chai (see page 156).

1. Wash the rice and soak overnight or for a minimum of 5–6 hours.
2. Drain and rinse the soaked rice, and blend with the coconut cream, milk, water, yeast and butter to form a smooth paste.
3. Pour the mixture into a large bowl. Add the sugar and cardamom. Cover and leave in a warm place to rise for 1 1/2–2 hours.
4. Put 1 Tbsp. (30 mL) of the ghee or butter in a frying pan about 12 inches (30 cm) in diameter. Place on high heat. When the ghee is hot, lower the heat to medium and pour in half of the mixture. Cook on low heat for 15 minutes until the mixture is set and the sides are golden.
5. Place the frying pan under a hot broiler for few minutes until the top becomes golden reddish brown. Repeat the process with the remaining mixture.
6. When it is completely cool, cut the Mkate into small squares and serve.

Serves 8–10

Parathas

A richer, softer and flakier variation of chapatis is a griddle-cooked bread called Paratha.

1. Sift the flour into a large bowl then add the salt and oil. Mix well.
2. Add enough water to make a soft elastic dough that is not sticky when kneaded.
3. Divide the dough into 8 balls.
4. On a floured surface roll out each ball thinly (approximately 8 inches/20 cm in diameter). Brush paratha surface with oil; sprinkle lightly with flour.
5. Fold in half, then in half again. Roll out thinly. Brush surface again with oil and sprinkle lightly with flour.
6. Heat a griddle on medium heat and cook one paratha at a time placing a little oil along the edges.
7. Cook the paratha on each side until golden brown. Serve hot.

Serve with Butter Chicken (page 51).

Makes 8

2 1/2 cups	whole-wheat flour	600 mL
1/2 tsp.	salt	2.5 mL
1/4 cup	vegetable oil	60 mL
3/4 cup	water	180 mL
2 Tbsp.	vegetable oil (for brushing)	30 mL
	whole-wheat flour (for sprinkling)	

Potato Parathas

Potato parathas make an excellent accompaniment for any curry. Although my family greatly enjoys them with fish and chicken curry, they are equally good with vegetable curries for all the vegetarians out there. They can also be served as appetizers, either hot or cold. Don't expect to have many leftovers.

4 ¼ cups	all-purpose flour	1 L
2 Tbsp.	instant yeast	30 mL
1 tsp.	salt	5 mL
½ tsp.	oregano (dried or fresh)	2.5 mL
¼ cup + 1 Tbsp.	vegetable oil	60 mL + 15 mL
2 cups	warm water	475 mL
1	large onion	1
¼ tsp.	haldi (turmeric)	1.2 mL
¼ tsp.	garlic (crushed)	1.2 mL
½ tsp.	salt	2.5 mL
¼ tsp.	chili powder or green chilies	1.2 mL
4	medium potatoes (boiled, peeled and mashed)	4
¼ cup	oil for frying	60 mL

1. Mix the flour, yeast, salt and oregano together in a mixing bowl.
2. Mix ¼ cup (60 mL) of the oil with the water in a small container. Pour the liquid into the dry ingredients to form a pizza-like dough. Set aside and let rise for 30 minutes.
3. Use the remaining 1 Tbsp. (15 mL) oil to cook the onion for about 10 minutes. Add the rest of the ingredients and stir well. Cook for 2 minutes.
4. Let cool for 10 minutes. Knead the dough lightly and divide into 10–12 balls.
5. Roll each ball into a 5-inch (12.5-cm) round. Place about ½ Tbsp. (7.5 mL) potato mix in the center and pinch the edges together to seal in the mix.
6. Roll out again gently, taking care not to squeeze the mix out, to 7–8 inch (17.5–20 cm) rounds.
7. Heat about 1 tsp. (5 mL) oil on medium high and fry paratha, turning until brown patches appear on each side. Repeat for remaining parathas.
8. Set aside on a plate covered with a tea cloth, and repeat above procedure for the remaining parathas.

Serve hot.

Serves 10–12

Simply Indian

Dahi Parathas

*D*ahi Parathas make a delicious accompaniment for any daal dish. My daughter, Safinaaz, enjoys her daal and Dahi Parathas with a side dish of tangy lemon pickles. If they are prepared ahead of time, wrapping them in foil and placing them inside a warm oven will keep them soft and moist. Dahi Parathas can also be frozen in foil.

4 cups	all-purpose flour	950 mL
½ cup	vegetable oil	120 mL
1 tsp.	sugar	5 mL
1 tsp.	baking powder	5 mL
½ tsp.	salt	2.5 mL
1	egg (beaten)	1
½ cup	yogurt	120 mL
½ cup	all-purpose flour (for sprinkling)	120 mL
¼ cup	vegetable oil (for frying)	60 mL

1. Mix the flour with ½ cup (120 mL) oil, sugar, baking powder and salt.
2. Add the egg and yogurt. Knead to form dough. Set aside, covered, for 2 hours to elasticize.
3. Roll out the dough into 6 or 7 balls (golf-ball size or slightly bigger).
4. Flatten the balls and sprinkle lightly on both sides with flour.
5. Roll out to about 12 inches (30 cm) in diameter.
6. Cook on medium high in a frying pan using ½ Tbsp. (7.5 mL) of oil for each paratha.
7. Cook until slightly spotted on both sides.

Serve hot with the curry of your choice.

Makes 6–7

Yeast Dahi Parathas

2 ½ cups	all-purpose flour	600 mL
½ cup	yogurt	120 mL
1 tsp.	instant yeast	5 mL
½ cup	warm water	120 mL
2 Tbsp.	margarine	30 mL
1	egg (beaten)	1
1 tsp.	baking powder	5 mL
1 tsp.	sugar	5 mL
1 tsp.	salt	5 mL
	butter or oil (for frying)	

These Yeast Parathas, sometimes described as the jewel of all parathas, go particularly well with Butter Chicken (see page 51). They are a great hit in my cooking classes and are also one of my specialties at parties.

1. Mix together all the ingredients.
2. Knead thoroughly with fingertips.
3. Cover and let sit for one hour in a warm place until the dough doubles in size.
4. Punch dough down, turn out onto floured surface, and knead until smooth. Divide into 5 or 6 equal parts.
5. Roll each part into an even round circle of 9 inches (22.5 cm) in diameter.
6. Fry on a hot griddle, with minimal butter or oil, until brown spots appear on both sides.

Serves 5–6

Rice

Rice is without any doubt the most important cereal crop in the world and is the staple food of more than half the world's population. Even in India's northern and central regions where chapatis and naan are eaten, rice still features strongly, especially in festive pilaus and biryanis.

Different types of rice are suited to different kinds of dishes. The long thin grains of basmati rice are preferred for pilaus and biryanis, while medium and short grain rice is better for creamy rice and milky sweets.

Soaking the rice in cold water seems to improve the yield when it is cooked and gives longer, more separate grains. The amount of liquid required has therefore been adjusted according to each recipe. The best rice dish when cooked shows each grain of rice as separate, firm and fluffy with no hard center. When given the appropriate care and attention, it can be a real delicacy fit for the finest feast imaginable.

Two of the more exotic rice dishes of India and Pakistan are biryanis and pilaus. These dishes are served on auspicious festive occasions or to welcome guests.

The rice dishes in this book are well worth trying and will more than reward your efforts in the kitchen.

Bhagharay Chawal (Plain Fried Rice)

2 ½ cups	basmati rice	600 mL
1	small onion	1
¼ cup	vegetable oil	60 mL
½ tsp.	garlic paste	2.5 mL
1 tsp.	salt	5 mL
¼ tsp.	jeera (whole black cumin seeds)	1.2 mL
4	whole cloves	4
4	cardamom pods	4
4 cups	water	950 mL

Light, very tasty and easy to make, this dish is excellent on a hot summer day when cooking seems too much of a challenge. The recipe can always be doubled for a larger crowd.

1. Wash rice and leave to soak in fresh water for 20 minutes. Drain.
2. Peel and slice onion. In a heavy saucepan, on medium high heat, fry the onion in the oil.
3. Add the garlic paste and stir well.
4. Add the salt, cumin, cloves and cardamom pods. Fry well for 1 minute.
5. Add the rice and stir until the water evaporates (about 10 minutes).
6. Add the 4 cups (950 mL) water and cook until ¾ of the water evaporates. Mix well, cover and let simmer for 10 minutes or until rice is tender. The length of time required will vary with different kinds of rice.

Serve with Palak Paneer (see page 36).

Serves 3–4

Variation 1

Decorate the rice with green peas to make Green Pea Pilau.

Variation 2

Decorate the rice with small koftas (spiced meatballs) to make Kofta Pilau.

Variation 3

Decorate the rice with slices of hard-boiled eggs to make Egg Pilau.

Chicken Biryani

*B*iryani is the *royal dish amongst all the exotic rice dishes of India, and even today it remains "the dish" to serve on all auspicious occasions and festivals. In our household Biryani is mainly prepared on Eid day, weddings and weekends.*

1. Wash the rice and soak for 20–30 minutes.
2. Joint the chicken and cut into curry size slices.
3. Marinate in the yogurt, ginger, garlic, salt, chili powder and yellow food coloring for at least 30 minutes.
4. In a large pan, heat 5 Tbsp. (75 mL) of the vegetable oil to medium high. Chop the tomatoes and add them to the oil. Cook for 10 minutes. Add the chicken mixture and tomato purée. Cook for 15 minutes (or until chicken is tender). Add the crispy fried onions and boiled potatoes.
5. Soak the saffron in ½ cup (120 mL) of boiling water for 3 minutes and pour half of it over the chicken. Add the garam masala and lemon juice. Remove from heat.
6. Bring 3 cups (720 mL) of water to a boil in a large pan and simmer for 1–2 minutes with cardamom, cinnamon sticks and salt. Add the rice and cook until ready, approximately 10 minutes.
7. Drain the rice, spread a layer in a pan and top with fried onions. Repeat for 3 layers, ending with rice.
8. Now pour the rest of the saffron water and vegetable oil on top of the rice.

Serve the rice in a separate bowl from the chicken and accompany with Onion Salad (see page 103) or Kachumber (Indian Mixed Salad, page 101).

Serves 6

3 ½ cups	basmati rice	840 mL
2 lbs.	chicken	900 g
2 cups	yogurt	475 mL
1 tsp.	ginger (crushed)	5 mL
1 tsp.	garlic (crushed)	5 mL
½ tsp.	salt (or to taste)	2.5 mL
¼ tsp.	chili powder	1.2 mL
½ tsp.	yellow food coloring	2.5 mL
½ cup	vegetable oil	120 mL
2	medium tomatoes	2
2 tsp.	tomato purée	10 mL
3 cups	crispy fried onions, ½ cup (120 mL) reserved for Step 7 (see page 54)	720 mL
6	small boiled potatoes (peeled)	6
½ tsp.	saffron	2.5 mL
½ cup	boiling water	120 mL
1 tsp.	garam masala	5 mL
3 Tbsp.	fresh lemon juice	45 mL
3 cups	water	720 mL
4	cardamom pods	4
2	cinnamon sticks (2 inches/5 cm long)	2
1 tsp.	salt	5 mL

Smokey Chicken Rice
(Rice with the Aroma of Barbecue)

2 ½ cups	rice	600 mL
1 cup	yogurt	240 mL
½ tsp.	garlic	2.5 mL
2	medium tomatoes (crushed)	2
1 tsp.	salt	5 mL
1 tsp.	black pepper	5 mL
1 tsp.	saffron	5 mL
1 Tbsp.	tandoori masala	15 mL
1 tsp.	garlic ginger paste	5 mL
2 lbs.	chicken (cut into small pieces)	900 g
1	large onion	1
1 cup	green onions	240 mL
½ cup	vegetable oil	120 mL
1 Tbsp.	tomato paste	15 mL
½ cup	fried onions	120 mL
6 cups	water	1.5 L

This recipe has been passed down through my family by my grandmother. For a traditional look, garnish with a few slices of hard-boiled egg and chopped parsley.

1. Wash the rice and soak for 20 minutes.
2. Mix together the yogurt, garlic, crushed tomatoes, salt, pepper, saffron, tandoori masala and garlic ginger paste to form a marinade. Marinate the chicken for 1 hour.
3. In a pan on medium high, sauté the large onion and green onions in the vegetable oil. Remove ¼ cup (60 mL) and set aside for step 6. Add tomato paste to remaining onions and cook until all the liquid dries up.
4. Add the chicken and cook for 15 minutes on low heat, until the chicken is tender. Set aside.
5. In another saucepan on medium high, boil the rice in 6 cups (1.5 L) water until tender. Drain.
6. In an ovenproof casserole, spread ⅓ of the rice mixed with 1 Tbsp. (15 mL) fried onions and green onions. Sprinkle a little of the chicken mixture on top. Repeat the process, layering the rice and the onion mixture, finally topping with rice.
7. Place a lighted charcoal on some foil on top of the rice and pour a few drops of hot oil on the lighted charcoal. Cover with the lid of the casserole for a few minutes to get the smokey fragrance. Remove the charcoal.
8. Lightly fluff the rice before putting it in the oven to bake at 300°F (150°C) for half an hour.

Serve with Raita (see page 95).

Serves 4–6

Coorgese Vegetable Pilau

*T*hank you very much to Bindu for sharing this southern Indian recipe.

1. Wash the rice and leave to soak for 30 minutes.
2. Meanwhile, bring the water to a boil and add the salt, potatoes and carrots. Cook until tender.
3. Heat 3 Tbsp. (15 mL) of the oil in a large saucepan on medium high heat and fry half the onions and all the tomatoes. Then add the turmeric and ground spices and fry for 1 minute.
4. Now add the potatoes, carrots, peas, ½ cup (120 mL) of water and cilantro and cook for 3–4 minutes.
5. In another frying pan, heat the remaining 2 Tbsp. (30 mL) of oil and fry the rest of the onions with the cinnamon stick, crushed peppercorn and cardamom pods. Add the drained rice and fry well for 2 minutes.
6. Add the coconut milk, cover and cook for 15 minutes, or until rice is almost done.
7. Add the vegetable mixture and cook uncovered on low heat for 3 minutes.

Serve with Onion Salad (see page 103) and papadams.

Serves 5

2 ½ cups	basmati rice	600 mL
4 cups	water	950 mL
1 ½ tsp.	salt	7.5 mL
2	large potatoes (cubed)	2
2	medium carrots (chopped)	2
5 Tbsp.	vegetable oil	75 mL
2	medium onions (chopped)	2
3	large tomatoes (finely chopped)	3
½ tsp.	haldi (turmeric)	2.5 mL
1 Tbsp.	dhanna (coriander) (ground)	15 mL
1 Tbsp.	jeera (cumin) (ground)	15 mL
1 tsp.	garlic (ground)	5 mL
1 tsp.	ginger (ground)	5 mL
½ cup	green peas	120 mL
½ cup	water	120 mL
1	bunch of cilantro (chopped)	1
1	cinnamon stick (2 inches/5 cm)	1
½ tsp.	peppercorn (crushed)	2.5 mL
2	cardamom pods	2
3 cups	coconut milk	720 mL

 Papadams can be obtained at any East Indian grocery store.

Moghlai Pilau

2 cups	basmati rice	475 mL
4 cups	water	950 mL
1 tsp.	salt	5 mL
2	cinnamon sticks (2 inches/5 cm long)	2
2	cardamom pods	2
3	cloves	3
¼ cup	milk	60 mL
1 Tbsp.	sultanas or 5 prunes	15 mL
3 Tbsp.	butter	45 mL
2 Tbsp.	blanched and finely slivered almonds	30 mL

This carefully compiled recipe should satisfy even the fussiest of eaters.

1. Wash rice, then soak it in fresh water for 20 minutes.
2. Boil the water and add the salt, cinnamon sticks, cardamom pods and cloves. Boil for approximately 2 minutes.
3. Add the drained rice and cook until tender, approximately 10 minutes. Drain the rice and sprinkle with milk. Set aside in a large casserole.
4. In a frying pan, on medium high, fry the prunes or sultanas in the butter until they start to swell.
5. Remove fruit and use the same butter to fry the slivered almonds until they turn pink. Sprinkle the almonds and butter over the rice.
6. Toss the sultanas or prunes, butter and almonds into the rice. Warm in a moderate oven for 20–30 minutes.

Serve with your favorite chicken curry and Raita (see page 95).

Serves 6

Simply Indian

Mutton and Pea Pilau

his pilau has more flavor than a plain pilau and it is usually served as a special treat. It goes rather well with Carrot Pickles (page 96) or Raita (page 95).

1. Boil the mutton in the water with the ginger, garlic and salt for 15–20 minutes. Meanwhile collect together the cumin seeds, cardamom pods, cloves, peppercorns, cinnamon sticks, chopped onion and green chili in a bowl.
2. Microwave peas for 6 minutes.
3. In a pan, heat the oil on medium heat. Put the spices, onion and green chili in the pan. Cover immediately to preserve flavor.
4. Add the potatoes and let them cook for a few minutes. Add 5 cups (1.2 L) of meat broth from the mutton. If the broth has reduced to less than this add water to make up the required volume. Bring to a boil.
5. Add the peas and drained rice. Cook on medium high for approximately 15 minutes.
6. When all the liquid is absorbed in the rice, reduce heat completely and cover the pot. Let it cook for half an hour more.

Serve with Onion Salad (see page 103).

Serves 4

1 lb.	mutton	455 g
6 cups	water	1.5 L
1 tsp.	ginger (crushed)	5 mL
1 tsp.	garlic (crushed)	5 mL
1 tsp.	salt	5 mL
½ tsp.	jeera (cumin seeds)	2.5 mL
3	cardamom pods	3
2	cloves	2
6	peppercorns	6
3	cinnamon sticks (2 inches/5 cm long)	3
1	onion (chopped)	1
1	green chili (deseeded and chopped)	1
1 cup	frozen peas	240 mL
3 Tbsp.	oil	45 mL
3	potatoes (peeled and cut into small pieces)	3
3 cups	basmati rice (soaked for 20 minutes)	720 mL

Navrattan Pilau

2 cups	basmati rice	475 mL
1 cup	paneer (see page 35)	240 mL
1/2 cup	vegetable oil	120 mL
1	large onion (chopped)	1
3	green cardamom pods	3
3 Tbsp.	vegetable oil	45 mL
1 tsp.	jeera (cumin seeds) (roasted)	5 mL
1/2 tsp.	garlic paste	2.5 mL
1 cup	green peas (fresh or frozen)	240 mL
1/2 tsp.	salt	2.5 mL
1	green chili (chopped and deseeded)	1
3 1/2 cups	water	840 mL
1/2 tsp.	orange food coloring	2.5 mL
1/2 tsp.	yellow food coloring	2.5 mL
1/2 tsp.	green food coloring	2.5 mL
1/2 tsp.	saffron	2.5 mL
1/2 cup	almonds (broken)	120 mL
1/2 cup	cashews (broken)	120 mL

This is a very festive and decorative dish. You can add extra ingredients according to taste to give it that special personal touch.

1. Wash the rice and soak in fresh water for 30 minutes.
2. Fry the paneer in the oil until golden. Remove and set aside.
3. In the same pan, sauté the onion, add the cardamom and cumin seeds and garlic paste, and cook for 30 seconds.
4. If using frozen green peas, microwave for 7 minutes and then add to the above mixture with the salt and chili.
5. Add the water to the pan and bring to a boil. Add the drained rice and cook for 10–15 minutes or until rice is ready.
6. Drain and divide into 3 portions.
7. Tint each portion with a different food coloring. Add strands of saffron to the yellow rice.
8. Toss in the almonds and cashews. Mix the rice well before serving.

Serve with the salad of your choice.

Serves 4

Indian Spanish-Style Rice

A unique East Indian take on this Spanish dish. The ginger, garlic and chopped red chilies give it that spicy, zingy taste. Enjoy!

1. Boil and shred the chicken. You may use beef or mutton if you prefer.
2. In a large pan, heat the oil on medium high. Chop the green onions in rings. Add the stem side and then the white part to the oil. Stir until slightly limp.
3. Add the remaining vegetables, salt and pepper. Add one more red chili if you want it very hot. Add chili powder, ginger and garlic, and fry for 1 minute.
4. Then add the tomato paste and tomato sauce. Cook for 5 more minutes.
5. Add the stock, vinegar and chicken and simmer on low heat for 5 minutes. Vegetables should be half cooked and crunchy.

Serve on a bed of rice, decorating with chopped hard-boiled eggs and fried onions (if you wish).

Serves 4

1 lb.	chicken (or beef or mutton)	455 g
2 Tbsp.	vegetable oil	30 mL
1	bunch of green onions (chopped)	1
2	green bell peppers (chopped)	2
1	carrot (chopped) (optional)	1
2	red chilies (deseeded) (optional)	2
1 tsp.	salt	5 mL
1/2 tsp.	black pepper	2.5 mL
1 tsp.	red chili powder	5 mL
1/2 tsp.	ginger (crushed)	2.5 mL
1/2 tsp.	garlic (crushed)	2.5 mL
1/2 cup	tomato paste	120 mL
3/4 cup	tomato sauce	180 mL
1 cup	chicken stock	240 mL
2 Tbsp.	white vinegar	30 mL

Masala Bhaath

5 cups	long grain rice	1.2 L
3 Tbsp.	butter	45 mL
3 Tbsp.	vegetable oil	45 mL
3	large onions (sliced)	3
5	cardamom pods (bruised)	5
2	small cinnamon sticks (2 inches/5 cm long)	2
6	cloves	6
20	black peppercorns (whole)	20
1/2 tsp.	haldi (ground turmeric)	2.5 mL
5 cups	hot water	1.2 L
3 tsp.	salt	15 mL
1/2 cup	cashew nuts	120 mL
2	sprigs of limro (fresh curry leaves)	2
3	green chilies (deseeded and sliced)	3
2 tsp.	rai (black mustard seeds)	10 mL

For garnish:

1/4 cup	fried cashews	60 mL
2 tsp.	cilantro (chopped)	10 mL
1/2 cup	fresh coconut (grated)	120 mL

This spicy rice is often served as the finale to a festive meal. It also works as the accompaniment to curries and pickles.

1. Wash rice well and leave to drain in a colander for at least 30 minutes.
2. In a large heavy saucepan, heat half the butter and half the oil. Fry the onions, cardamom pods, cinnamon sticks, cloves and black pepper until the onions are golden brown, stirring frequently.
3. Remove half of the onions and set aside for garnish.
4. Add the turmeric and rice to the pan and fry, stirring with a slotted metal spoon until the grains are coated with butter.
5. Add the hot water and salt. Stir well and bring to a boil. Cover with tightly fitting lid and turn heat down to a gentle simmer. Cook for 15 minutes without lifting the lid.
6. Heat the remaining butter and oil in a small pan and fry the cashew nuts until golden. Remove from the pan with slotted spoon and set aside.
7. Fry the curry leaves, green chilies and mustard seeds until seeds pop. Pour over the rice, lightly fluffing rice with a fork.
8. Garnish with fried cashews, chopped cilantro and fresh grated coconut.

Serve with Carrot Pickles (see page 96).

Serves 6

Til Bhaath (Rice with Sesame Seeds)

Til Bhaath is very famous in southern India where it is often served with a piping hot bowl of curried vegetables. I can bet you this delightful dish will have guests coming back for seconds.

1. Put rice, water and salt into a heavy saucepan and boil on medium high heat for 5 minutes.
2. Cover with well-fitting lid, turn heat down to low and simmer for 20 minutes.
3. Turn off heat and leave aside while preparing seasoning.
4. Heat the sesame oil in a small saucepan over medium low heat and fry the mustard seeds and curry leaves until mustard seeds pop and leaves are brown.
5. Add the sesame seeds and keep stirring over medium heat until the seeds are evenly golden brown.
6. Mix this seasoning together with the hot cooked rice and add a little lemon juice to taste.

Serve with curried vegetables, fresh chutney and fried papadams.

Serves 4–6

2 ½ cups	long grain rice	600 mL
4 cups	water	950 mL
2 ½ tsp.	salt	12.5 mL
2 Tbsp.	light sesame oil	30 mL
1 tsp.	rai (black mustard seeds)	5 mL
12	limro (curry leaves)	12
1 cup	sesame seeds	240 mL
2 Tbsp.	fresh lemon juice	30 mL

Vegetable Rice
(Spiced Rice with Mixed Vegetables)

2 1/2 cups	basmati rice	600 mL
5 cups	water	1.2 L
1 1/2 tsp.	salt	7.5 mL
3 Tbsp.	vegetable oil	45 mL
1/4 cup	crispy fried onions (see page 54)	60 mL
1/2 tsp.	tomato paste	2.5 mL
1/2 tsp.	garlic (ground)	2.5 mL
pinch	salt	pinch
1/2 tsp.	garam masala	2.5 mL
1/2 tsp.	Fijian Mixed Spice (see page xi), plus pinch for layering	2.5 mL
1 cup	mixed frozen vegetables (microwaved for 6 minutes)	240 mL

Whenever I have large gatherings at my place, this is one of the dishes I always prepare. It is very simple, yet has a delicious combination of Fijian spices with rice and vegetables.

1. Clean the rice and soak in fresh water for 20 minutes.
2. In a heavy saucepan on medium high heat, bring the water to a boil. Add the rice and salt and cook until rice is almost ready (10–15 minutes).
3. In a frying pan, heat the oil and add half the onions, the tomato paste, garlic, pinch of salt, garam masala and Fijian Mixed Spice.
4. Add the microwaved vegetables to the pan and cook for 3 minutes.
5. Drain the rice and layer in a pan alternating layers with the mixed vegetables, pinch of Fijian Mixed Spice and remaining fried onions.
6. Place in oven at 300° (150°C) for 10–15 minutes.

Serve with Raita (page 95) and Tandoori Chicken (page 74).

Serves 5

Exotic Sweets and Drinks

One lasting memory of a trip to India is how wonderful the drinks were and how appropriate each one was to my needs. A very popular beverage throughout India is Masala Chai. There is no substitute for a drink on a hot day, whether it is a sweet or salty Lassi, or the famous deliciously chilled Faluda drink.

Every East Indian should be proud of the exotic and mouth-watering sweets from the different parts of India. There are literally dozens of varieties of sweetmeats in East Indian cooking. Many of them have been passed down from generation to generation. Most are based on concentrated milk products, almonds, or lentils due to their cooling properties.

This chapter introduces a range of traditional sweets—some are easy to make for beginners and others are more intricate for the experienced chefs. Enjoy finding your personal favorite.

Badaam Paak

2 cups	slivered almonds	475 mL
4 cups	milk (homogenized is best)	950 mL
1 cup	sugar	240 mL
1/4 tsp.	saffron	1.2 mL
1/4 lb.	unsalted butter	113 g
1 tsp.	cardamom powder	5 mL

A mouth-watering dessert that is sure to impress your guests, especially when served cold.

1. Put almonds in blender with 2 1/2 cups (600 mL) of the milk. Blend coarsely.
2. Wash blender out with the remaining milk and pour all of it in a nonstick pan with the sugar, saffron and butter.
3. Bring to a boil on medium high and stir continuously for 45 minutes. When the mixture thickens, add the cardamom powder.
4. Grease a baking tray (10 inches x 14 inches/25 cm x 35 cm) and pour the mixture into it and flatten it out.
5. Let cool and cut into small squares.

Serves 6–7

Simply Indian

Shahi Tukre

This dessert of the Nawabis is without a doubt India's most exotic and well-known sweet dish, garnished with nuts and covered with edible silver sheets. Yum!

1. Cut the bread into thick slices and fry in butter on medium high heat until light golden brown.
2. Boil the milk on low heat until it reduces to 2 cups (475 mL).
3. Add the sugar and bring back to boiling point.
4. Put in the fried bread and cook gently to soak up most of the milk.
5. Add the rosewater and cardamom powder. Lay bread in serving dish and cover with cream.
6. Sprinkle chopped nuts on top and also a few rose petals and silver foil.
7. Cut into slices to serve.

Serves 4

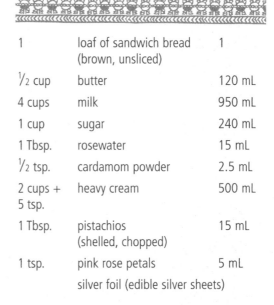

1	loaf of sandwich bread (brown, unsliced)	1
½ cup	butter	120 mL
4 cups	milk	950 mL
1 cup	sugar	240 mL
1 Tbsp.	rosewater	15 mL
½ tsp.	cardamom powder	2.5 mL
2 cups + 5 tsp.	heavy cream	500 mL
1 Tbsp.	pistachios (shelled, chopped)	15 mL
1 tsp.	pink rose petals	5 mL
	silver foil (edible silver sheets)	

 Edible silver foil can be obtained at all East Indian grocery stores. Rosewater can be found in large grocery stores—or try any Iranian or East Indian grocery store.

Sev Laddu

¼ cup	slivered almonds	60 mL
¼ cup	pistachios (shelled)	60 mL
1 cup	milk powder	240 mL
¾ cup	condensed milk	180 mL
¼ cup	ghee (clarified butter)	60 mL
1 lb.	thin sev (vermicelli)	455 g
1 tsp.	cardamom (crushed)	5 mL

Absolutely delicious—and quick and easy to make.

1. Mix together the nuts, milk powder and condensed milk in a bowl.
2. Heat the ghee or butter in a pan on medium high heat. Fry the sev, stirring continuously until golden brown.
3. Remove from heat and mix with the milk and nuts. Sprinkle cardamom over top.
4. Make small round laddus of golf ball size or bigger. You should have between 20 and 25 balls.

Makes 20–25

 Thin sev (vermicelli) is found in East Indian grocery stores. Do not mix this up with thin angel hair pasta or any other pasta.

Simply Indian

Rasgullas

*E*very happy occasion of Indian life revolves around sweets, be it birth, marriage, or any good news. Make this treat a part of your own special occasions.

1. Boil the milk and add the lemon juice gradually until the milk curdles.
2. Pour the curdled milk into a muslin cloth, tie up and hang for at least 3 hours to drain the water completely.
3. The contents will look like cottage cheese. Knead gently for about 10–15 minutes, until it becomes soft and smooth.
4. Add the flour and baking powder and continue rubbing.
5. Form into 14–16 balls.
6. Boil the sugar in the water. Add the 1 Tbsp. (15 mL) of milk and the cheese balls and continue to boil on high for 15 minutes.
7. Let the Rasgullas cool for 2–3 hours before serving and add the rose essence.

Serves 6–7

10 cups	milk	2.4 L
2 Tbsp.	lemon juice (fresh or bottled)	30 mL
1 cup	all-purpose flour	240 mL
¼ tsp.	baking powder	1.2 mL
2 cups	sugar	475 mL
5 cups	water	1.2 L
1 Tbsp.	milk	15 mL
¼ tsp.	rose essence (see page 154)	1.2 mL
	few drops food coloring (optional, see below)	

Helpful Hint:
You can add a few drops of the food coloring of your choice to the cottage cheese mixture at step 3 to get different colored Rasgullas.

Rasmalai

Basic ingredients:

1 cup	milk powder	240 mL
1 tsp.	baking powder	5 mL
1	egg (beaten)	1
1 Tbsp.	vegetable oil	15 mL
1 Tbsp.	all-purpose flour	15 mL

For the milk syrup:

½ cup	sugar	120 mL
2	cardamom pods (ground)	2
1 cup	evaporated milk	240 mL
3 cups	fresh milk (homogenized)	720 mL
	chopped almonds and pistachios to decorate	
	ground cardamom and saffron threads (optional)	

*T*his dessert is perfect for special occasions—and for those who have a sweet tooth. I have included 3 versions. All are easy to make and can be refrigerated for up to 1 week.

Method for dough:
1. Mix basic ingredients by hand to form a dough. Make walnut-sized (or slightly smaller) balls.
2. The balls should be made immediately, before the dough becomes dry.

Method for syrup:
1. In a large saucepan, boil the syrup ingredients on medium high.
2. While this is boiling, drop in the balls and cook, partly covered, for 5–8 minutes. Do not cover fully or milk will boil over.
3. When the balls have doubled in size, take them out and put them into a glass bowl. Pour over the milk syrup.
4. Decorate with chopped almonds and pistachios. You may also add ground cardamon and saffron threads.

Chill before serving.

Serves 6

Variation 1—Rasmalai with Vermicelli

1. Should anything go wrong with your main Rasmalai recipe, and you don't get the intended results then you may crush the Rasmalai balls.
2. Boil 1 cup (240 mL) vermicelli in 2 cups (475 mL) of milk, mix in the crushed Rasmalai and boil for 2 minutes.
3. Let cool to produce a delicious dessert—Rasmalai with Vermicelli.

Serves 6

Basic ingredients plus:

1 cup	vermicelli	240 mL
2 cups	milk	475 mL

Variation 2—Rasmalai with Ricotta Cheese

1. In a saucepan, on medium high heat, quickly dry the ricotta cheese and ¼ tsp. (1.2 mL) of saffron, stirring continuously.
2. Pour the mixture into a casserole dish and bake for 10–20 minutes at 300°F (150°).
3. When it starts to turn brown at the edges, remove from the oven and set aside.
4. In another saucepan, on medium high heat, boil the half-and-half with the remaining saffron, cardamom powder, evaporated milk and sugar. Boil for 10 minutes then pour over the baked cheese. Cut into small squares.
5. Refrigerate and serve the next day.

Serves 6

Basic ingredients plus:

18 oz.	ricotta cheese	500 g
½ tsp.	saffron	2.5 mL
1 cup	half-and-half	250 mL
¼ tsp.	cardamom powder	1.2 mL
1 ⅔ cups	evaporated milk	400 mL
5–6 Tbsp.	sugar	75–90 mL

Pineapple Halwa

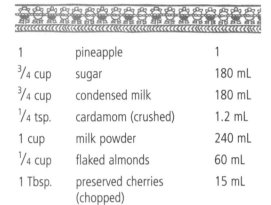

1	pineapple	1
³/₄ cup	sugar	180 mL
³/₄ cup	condensed milk	180 mL
¹/₄ tsp.	cardamom (crushed)	1.2 mL
1 cup	milk powder	240 mL
¹/₄ cup	flaked almonds	60 mL
1 Tbsp.	preserved cherries (chopped)	15 mL

*E*njoy this old-time family favorite and watch it disappear before your very eyes.

1. Cut the pineapple lengthwise in two. Keep one half with its shell and leaves.
2. Remove the flesh from both halves of the pineapple. Use a spoon to scoop out the flesh from the shell you are keeping and cube the flesh from the other half.
3. Put all the flesh into a saucepan.
4. Add the sugar and cook on high heat until all the liquid dries up. Stir continuously so that it does not burn.
5. Add the condensed milk and cardamom. Stir well and cook for 8 minutes.
6. Add milk powder and almonds. Mix and cook for a couple of minutes. Remove and cool.
7. Pour the halwa into the shell with leaves, garnish with chopped cherries and serve.

Serves 4

Pera

This is a sweetmeat for all seasons.

1. Over low heat, melt the butter or margarine then add the evaporated milk.
2. When the milk comes to a boil, add the sugar and stir until sticky.
3. Add the rest of the ingredients.
4. Mix well and cook until oil starts to separate from the mixture.
5. Remove from the heat and cool for a few minutes.
6. Roll into approximately 8–10 balls and allow to set.

Serves 4–5

3 oz.	butter or margarine	90 g
1 cup	evaporated milk	240 mL
³/₄ cup	sugar	180 mL
1 tsp.	cardamom (crushed)	5 mL
1 tsp.	nutmeg (powdered)	5 mL
¹/₄ tsp.	saffron	1.2 mL

Jardo (Sweet Colorful Rice)

Jardo is made for special occasions and is often decorated with pistachios, almonds and pounded silver papers (warq). It is best when served hot, but also good when cold.

1. Boil the rice in 3 cups (720 mL) water for 7 minutes, then drain off any water. The rice should be half cooked.
1. In a heavy saucepan on medium low fry the sugar, crushed cardamom and raisins in butter for 1 minute. Add the water and a drop of orange color. Add the rice and chopped almonds. Mix gently.
2. Make holes in the rice with the end of the spoon. Put 2–3 drops of color in each hole. Cover and cook on a very low heat for 5 minutes more.
3. Mix it well before serving.

Serves 6–8

2 cups	rice	475 mL
2 cups	sugar	475 mL
1 tsp.	cardamom (crushed)	5 mL
¹/₄ cup	sultanas or other raisins	60 mL
4 oz.	butter	113 g
1 cup	water	240 mL
	few drops of orange, red and green food colorings	
¹/₂ cup	almonds (boiled for 2–3 minutes, peeled and chopped)	120 mL

Mung Daal Halwa

4 cups	mung daal	950 mL
½ tsp.	saffron	2.5 mL
2 Tbsp.	hot water	30 mL
2 cups	butter or ghee	475 mL
2 cups	sugar	475 mL
10 cups	milk	2.4 L
1 tsp.	cardamom powder	5 mL
1 Tbsp.	flaked almonds	15 mL
2 Tbsp.	cashew nuts	30 mL

This is a popular version of the rich halwa seen on the menus of many Indian restaurants.

1. Soak the mung daal overnight. Next day rinse twice in water, drain and blend to make a fine paste (try not to use too much water).
2. Soak saffron in the hot water for 3 minutes.
3. Using 1 ½ cups (360 mL) of the butter or ghee, fry the paste on low heat in a wok for at least 1 hour, stirring frequently, until color changes to pink, all the water has evaporated and the ghee rises to the top.
4. Add the sugar and milk and, still on low heat, cook for another 15 minutes, stirring continuously.
5. When the mixture dries up again add the remaining butter or ghee, the cardamon, half of the almonds and the saffron water.
6. Remove from heat and pour into a medium-sized dish. Decorate with the remaining nuts.

Serve either warm or cold.

Serves 3–4

Monthal

Monthal was traditionally prepared only during festive and wedding occasions. Nowadays, success in anything sparks a demand for sweetmeats. Guests are offered them as a welcome and a sign of hospitality.

1. Heat the evaporated milk. Add the 1 cup (240 mL) ghee or butter and mix in the flour until it looks like dry breadcrumbs.

2. Make a thick syrup from the sugar and water. To check whether the syrup is ready, put a drop on a plate. If it is firm and does not spread, it is ready. Keep warm by putting a lid on the saucepan.

3. In a big pot, heat the 8 oz. (225 g) butter and 1 lb. (455 g) ghee and fry the flour and milk mix until it is a golden brown color. Add the food coloring and syrup.

4. Mix together the milk powder, cardamom, nutmeg and saffron and add to the pot.

5. Mix well. Pour onto a deep cookie sheet and decorate with almonds, pistachios, poppy seeds and some nutmeg. After 4 hours cut it in diamond or square shapes.

Makes 15–18 pieces

1 cup	evaporated milk	240 mL
1 cup	ghee or butter	240 mL
2 lbs.	gram flour	1 kg
2 lbs.	sugar	1 kg
3 cups	water	720 mL
8 oz.	butter	225 g
1 lb.	ghee	455 g
1/2 tsp.	yellow food coloring	2.5 mL
1 lb.	milk powder	455 g
1 tsp.	cardamom	5 mL
1 Tbsp.	nutmeg (powdered)	15 mL
1 tsp.	saffron	5 mL
1 cup	chopped almonds	240 mL
1 cup	chopped pistachios	240 mL
2 Tbsp.	white poppy seeds	30 mL
	extra nutmeg to decorate	

Laddoo

Ingredients for dumplings :

1 lb.	gram flour	455 g
1/2 cup	melted ghee or clarified butter	120 mL
1/2	can (7 oz./190 mL) evaporated milk	1/2
1/4 tsp.	yellow food coloring	1.2 mL
2 cups	water	475 mL
2 lbs.	ghee (for deep-frying)	900 g
4 oz.	blanched almonds (slivered)	113 g
3 oz.	pistachios (slivered)	85 g
4 oz.	raisins or sultanas	113 g
1/4 cup	cardamom seeds (crushed)	60 mL

This very popular Indian sweetmeat is a must for wedding celebrations and any joyous occasion in both the Muslim and Hindu communities.

Method for dumplings:

1. Sift the gram flour into a medium bowl, add melted ghee, evaporated milk, food coloring and water. Make a smooth batter, slightly thicker than pancake batter.
2. Now heat the 2 lbs. (900 g) ghee in a wok on medium high heat. Hold an aluminum colander or "jara" over the wok and pour 1–2 cups (240-475 mL) of batter in it. Shake the colander or stir with a wooden spoon so the drops of batter will fall into the wok to make dumplings. Fry the dumplings for 2 minutes. Remove and put aside. Repeat the process to produce dumplings from the remaining batter until the batter is used up.
3. Blend dumplings in food processor to coarsely crush them. Alternatively, you may crush the dumplings between your palms.
4. Fry almonds and pistachios for 1 minute in the same ghee on medium heat.
5. Remove ghee, keeping 1–2 cups (240–475 mL) to fry raisins on medium heat until they become plump. Remove the raisins and set aside.
6. Combine the crushed dumplings with the cardamom, almonds, pistachios and raisins.

Method for sugar syrup:

1. Put water, sugar, food coloring and saffron in a large saucepan. Mix with a wooden spoon.

2. Keep this on medium high heat and let it boil, stirring occasionally, for 15 minutes.

3. Make the syrup foamy and sticky and thick to only 1 thread (see page vii). To check the thickness of the syrup, just place one drop between your first two fingers. Part the fingers to check the thread. Remove from heat.

4. Add the dumpling mixture to this syrup and mix thoroughly so that all the syrup is absorbed.

5. Heat the remaining ghee and pour 1 cup (240 mL) over the dumplings. Let cool for 10 minutes. Form into balls the size of table tennis balls, or smaller if you wish.

Makes 15–20

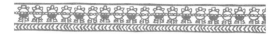

Ingredients for sugar syrup:

2 cups	water	475 mL
1 3/4 lbs.	sugar	800 g
1/4 tsp.	yellow food coloring	1.2 mL
1 tsp.	saffron	5 mL

Mesoob (Exotic Milk Fudge)

1 ¼ lbs.	sugar	565 g
1 cup	water	240 mL
¼ tsp.	yellow food coloring	1.2 mL
1 ½ lbs.	ghee or clarified butter	680 g
1 lb.	gram flour	455 g
¼ cup	milk	60 mL

*A*nother popular exotic Indian sweetmeat. Eaten hot or cold, it is a gourmet's delight.

1. In a saucepan, make a syrup by heating the water and sugar over low heat. Bring to a boil then simmer and add yellow food coloring while simmering.
2. In a wok, heat 1 cup (240 mL) of the ghee and fry the flour on medium low heat for 5–8 minutes. Start pouring in the hot ghee and syrup little by little, stirring continuously until the mixture starts foaming and oozing out the ghee.
3. Continue to add the ghee. When the mixture is frothy and leaving the pan, remove from heat. Pour in a tray and sprinkle milk on top.
4. Cut into diamond shapes or any shape you prefer.
5. Serve and savor.

Makes 20–25

Simply Indian

Kibibi (Sweet Rice Pancakes)

K ibibi is a specialty of the island of Zanzibar. It tastes almost like Vitumbua (see page 151) and Mkate (see page 116) but it is much easier to make. The pancakes taste best when eaten plain.

1. Wash the rice thoroughly and soak overnight in fresh water.
2. Blend soaked rice with the coconut milk and fresh milk to form a smooth and runny batter.
3. Add the sugar, yeast and cardamom. Pour into a large bowl.
4. Cover and place somewhere warm to rise for 2 hours.
5. Heat a nonstick frying pan on medium high and grease with vegetable oil.
6. Using a ladle, pour the batter to make thin pancakes.
7. Cover with a lid for about 1 minute.
8. Remove when the bottom of the pancake is golden brown. The top of the pancake should still be white.
9. Repeat with the remaining batter.
10. Keep the cooked pancakes warm on a plate by covering with a tea towel.

Makes 20

2 cups	rice (soaked overnight)	475 mL
1 cup	coconut milk (thick)	240 mL
¾ cup	milk	180 mL
1 cup	sugar	240 mL
2 tsp.	instant yeast	10 mL
1 tsp.	cardamom (crushed)	5 mL
3 Tbsp.	vegetable oil (for frying)	45 mL

Kheer (Sweet Rice Pudding)

1/2 cup	basmati rice (soaked overnight)	120 mL
4 cups	half-and-half	950 mL
1 1/4 cups	sugar	360 mL
1/4 tsp.	nutmeg (powdered)	1.2 mL
1/4 tsp.	cardamom	1.2 mL
1/4 tsp.	saffron	1.2 mL
1/4 cup	each almonds and pistachios (chopped)	60 mL
4 cups	whipping cream	950 mL

*K*heers are very rich dishes and are normally reserved for special occasions. They are often decorated with coarsely ground almonds and pistachios and pounded silver papers (warq), which are edible and very attractive.

1. Drain the rice and break it up with your hands into smaller grains.
2. Add to the half-and-half in a saucepan, and bring to a boil for 30 minutes, stirring continuously so that it does not stick. Reduce heat.
3. Beat with an electric mixer while still on low heat.
4. Add the sugar, nutmeg, cardamom and saffron and some of the almonds.
5. Add the whipping cream and let simmer for a few minutes.
6. Pour into a serving dish and decorate with pistachios and almonds.

Serve with puris (page 109–113).

Serves 4–5

Jalebi (Batter Coils in Syrup)

Jalebis are the children's finger-licking favorites. The secret of this sweet is to eat it soon after cooking, when it is hot and crispy. These sweetmeats are dipped into syrup and are suitable for any occasion.

1. Mix the flours with the yogurt, yeast and water to form a thick creamy batter. Set aside, covered, for 2 hours to ferment. Whisk thoroughly before using.

2. Make a one string syrup by dissolving sugar in water and bring to a boil (see page vii). Just before the syrup is ready, add the saffron and crushed cardamom seeds.

3. Heat oil in a frying pan on medium heat. Pour batter through a small funnel (or a coconut shell with a hole) into the frying pan and move the batter round to form coils. Deep-fry these for 30 seconds to ensure they are crisp and golden but not brown.

4. Remove from pan and drain on paper towels then immerse into syrup. Leave for 3–4 minutes so they soak up as much syrup as possible.

Serve hot (if possible).

Makes 20–25

Batter ingredients:

1 ½ cups	all-purpose flour	360 mL
½ cup	gram flour	120 mL
½ cup	yogurt	120 mL
¼ tsp.	yeast	1.2 mL
1 cup	water	240 mL

Syrup ingredients:

1 cup	sugar	240 mL
1 ½ cups	water	360 mL
¼ tsp.	saffron	1.2 mL
½ tsp.	green cardamom seeds (crushed)	2.5 mL
3 cups	vegetable oil (for deep-frying)	720 mL

 Please read "Before You Begin" (page vii) before starting to make the syrup.

Barfi

A moist and tasty treat. Superb with any Indian dish, like Chicken Biryani (page 123).

1 cup + 1 Tbsp.	whipping cream	255 mL
1/2 cup	sugar	120 mL
1 1/2 Tbsp.	butter	22.5 mL
3 cups	powdered milk	720 mL
1 tsp.	cardamom powder	5 mL
1/2 tsp.	vanilla essence	2.5 mL

1. Bring whipping cream to a boil. Mix in the sugar and butter. Boil for approximately 10 minutes, stirring occasionally.
2. Add powdered milk a little at a time with the cardamom powder. Remove from heat then add vanilla essence.
3. Pour on greased pan (medium-sized cookie sheet is fine). Let cool and become hard.
4. Cut into diamond shapes and refrigerate.

Makes 20

Vitumbua

This dish comes from the Indians in East Africa who originated from Zanzibar. Vitumbua are usually served as breakfast and in the month of Ramadan they are served as an appetizer when breaking fast. The women in Zanzibar prepare this early in the afternoon to sell at market.

1. Wash rice thoroughly and soak overnight in fresh water.
2. Blend the soaked rice with the coconut milk and fresh milk to a smooth paste.
3. Add sugar, instant yeast and cardamom. Pour mixture into a large bowl.
4. Cover and leave in a warm place to rise for 2 hours.
5. Heat a kitumbua karai on medium heat. Add ½ tsp. (2.5 mL) of the vegetable oil.
6. Mix batter with a ladle and pour one large spoon of the mixture in the kitumbua karai and fry for 2–3 minutes. Turn with a fork and let it sit for another 2–3 minutes. Remove when golden brown.
7. Repeat with the remaining batter, adding oil only when required.

Can be served hot or cold.

Makes 12

2 cups	rice (soaked overnight)	475 mL
1 cup	coconut milk (thick)	240 mL
½ cup	milk	120 mL
1 cup	sugar	240 mL
2 tsp.	instant yeast	10 mL
1 tsp.	cardamom (crushed)	5 mL
3 Tbsp.	vegetable oil (for frying)	45 mL

 Kitumbua karai is a special griddle that has a round depression like a cup cake tray. I have not found an alternative piece of equipment for this.

Luxury Trifle

1/2 lb.	butter	225 g
5 oz.	brown sugar	140 g
1 lb.	plain cake (cut into pieces)	455 g
1 lb.	fresh or canned pineapple	455 g
4 cups	custard	950 mL
1 cup	clotted cream	240 mL
	fruit (your choice) to decorate	

Clotted cream is a very thick, rich cream. Look for it in your grocer's dairy section. It's often called Devonshire or Devon cream.

A lovely combination of caramelized cake, custard and cream with pineapple. This extraordinary trifle is a favorite of my daughter-in-law, Aarifa. Ready-made custard is available in grocery stores.

1. Heat butter on medium low and add the brown sugar. Add cake and allow to caramelize. Mix well and let cool.
2. Take a large glass bowl, add 1/4 of the caramelized cake and place pineapple pieces on top. Repeat the process 3 times more and then pour over all the remaining pineapple syrup. If using fresh pineapple, the juice from the pineapple should be used as the syrup.
3. Pour the custard over top and spread over the clotted cream. Decorate with fruit or angelica and cherries.
4. Chill and serve cold.

Serves 8

Apple Blossom Punch

10 cups	frozen orange juice (keep frozen)	2.4 L
2 cups	apple juice	475 mL
2 cups	ginger ale	475 mL
4 cups	ice cubes	950 mL
2	orange slices	2

1. Mix the orange and apple juice in a pitcher and chill.
2. Add ginger ale and ice cubes when ready to serve.
3. Garnish with orange slices.

Simply Indian

Cranberry Punch

1. Mix together the cranberry juice, lemonade and orange juice. Chill.
2. Just before serving, add gingerale, ice cubes, frozen strawberries and cherries into the serving jug.

8 cups	cranberry juice	2 L
3 cups	frozen lemonade (keep frozen)	720 mL
3 cups	frozen orange juice (keep frozen)	720 mL
8 cups	ginger ale	2 L
4 cups	ice cubes	950 mL
½ cup	frozen strawberries	120 mL
½ cup	maraschino cherries	120 mL

Homemade Vimto

Perfect on a hot day.

1. Make a syrup by boiling water and sugar until sticky, producing 2 strains between two fingers (see page vii).
2. Add potash essence and citric acid.
3. Cool and store in a bottle.
4. Add 6–8 cups (1.5–2 L) cold water. Stir and serve.

Serves 10–12

3 cups	water	720 mL
3 cups	sugar	720 mL
3 Tbsp.	potash essence	45 mL
3 tsp.	citric acid (lemon flower)	15 mL

Potash essence can be found at your local East Indian grocery store. It can be difficult to track down as it tends to sell very quickly.

Faluda Drink (Cold Vermicelli Drink)

4 oz.	faluda sev or any thick vermicelli	200 g
½ tsp.	green food coloring	2.5 mL
½ tsp.	red food coloring	2.5 mL
16 cups	milk (homogenized)	4 L
1 cup	sugar	240 mL
1 tsp.	rose essence	5 mL
1	large can (14 oz./385 mL) evaporated milk	1
½ tsp.	pink food coloring	2.5 mL
2 Tbsp.	takhmaria seeds (soaked in 2 cups/475 mL of water)	30 mL
	vanilla ice cream	
1 cup	rose syrup	240 mL

Rose essence and rose syrup can be obtained at your local supermarket in the baking section. Takhmaria seeds are derived from the tulsi tree, which only grows in tropical countries. The seeds can be found in small packages in East Indian grocery stores.

There are many versions of Faluda. This one is a favorite of mine. It is a sweet drink for serving with spicy meals. It gets its name from the particles of cornflower vermicelli that float in it. Faluda can be served as a dessert or simply as a refreshing drink.

1. Divide the faluda sev in two and boil each section separately, adding ½ tsp. (2.5 mL) green food coloring into one and ½ tsp. (2.5 mL) red food coloring into the other. Drain and put each into a separate bowl.
2. Boil milk for 20 minutes, stirring continuously. Add sugar, rose essence, evaporated milk and pink food coloring. Let cool.
3. Add soaked takhmaria and chill.
4. Half-fill a tall glass with the chilled milk, then add the following: 1 scoop of ice cream, ½ tsp. (2.5 mL) each of green and red faluda sev, and then 1 Tbsp. (15 mL) of rose syrup.

Serve with a drinking straw.

Serves 15–20

Lassi

There is no substitute for this very popular drink, either here in Indian restaurants or back in India. It is very refreshing and, when served with hot spicy foods, it aids digestion.

1. Combine the yogurt, cumin, salt and pepper in a jug and whisk vigorously with a balloon whisk until the mixture is smooth.
2. Add the crushed ice and water and continue to whisk for 1 minute.
3. Refrigerate and serve chilled.

Serves 4

Salted Lassi

2 cups	yogurt	475 mL
1/2 tsp.	roasted jeera (cumin) (coarsely ground)	2.5 mL
3/4 tsp.	salt	4 mL
1/4 tsp.	ground black pepper	1.2 mL
1 cup	crushed ice	240 mL
2 cups	cold water	475 mL

1. Combine the yogurt, sugar, salt, mint leaves and pepper in a jug and whisk vigorously with a balloon whisk until the mixture is smooth.
2. Add the crushed ice and water and continue to whisk for 1 minute.
3. Refrigerate and serve chilled.

Serves 4

Sweet Lassi

2 cups	yogurt	475 mL
1/4 cup	sugar	60 mL
1/4 tsp.	salt	1.2 mL
1/2 tsp.	dried mint leaves	2.5 mL
1/4 tsp.	ground black pepper	1.2 mL
1 cup	crushed ice	240 mL
2 cups	cold water	475 mL

Masala Chai

A spicy tea that is ideal for cold, wintry days.

2 cups	water	475 mL
2 Tbsp.	sugar	30 mL
3	tea bags	3
1	cardamom pod	1
1	cinnamon stick (about ½ inch/1.2 cm)	1
1	pinch of nutmeg	1
1	pinch of ginger	1
1 cup	milk	240 mL

1. Combine all ingredients except the milk in a pot and bring to a boil for 3–5 minutes.
2. Add the milk, stir gently for another 3 minutes, reduce heat and continue to cook for another 3 minutes.

Serve immediately while hot.

Serves 3

Mixed Fruit Punch

3 Tbsp.	passion fruit juice	45 mL
3 Tbsp.	orange juice	45 mL
2 Tbsp.	rose syrup	30 mL
3 cups	soda water	720 mL
1 Tbsp.	mint leaves	15 mL
1	apple (peeled and chopped)	1
½ cup	strawberries (chopped)	120 mL
6–7 cups	cold water	1.5–1.75 L

1. Mix together the juices with the syrup and soda water.
2. Add mint leaves and chopped fruit, stirring gently to mix.
3. Add cold water and serve.

Serves 6–8

Mohit Sharbat

This sharbat is very popular amongst athletes for its refreshing properties.

1. Squeeze the juice from the lemons into a large deep bowl.
2. Add the sugar and water and whisk vigorously for 2–3 minutes.
3. Add the kewra essence and crushed ice and stir continuously for 1 minute.
4. Serve immediately in long glasses garnished with a slice of lemon.

Serves 5

2	large lemons	2
³/₄ cup	sugar	180 mL
2 ¹/₂ cups	water	600 mL
¹/₂ tsp.	kewra essence	2.5 mL
¹/₂ cup	crushed ice	120 mL
4	lemon slices (round and thin)	4

 Kewra essence can be obtained at any East Indian grocery store.

Exotic Sweets and Drinks

Index